ONLINE DANGER

ONLINE
DANGER

HOW TO PROTECT YOURSELF
AND YOUR LOVED ONES FROM
THE EVIL SIDE
OF THE INTERNET

DR. ERIC COLE
(ONLINE SECURITY EXPERT AND CYBER NINJA)

NEW YORK

LONDON • NASHVILLE • MELBOURNE • VANCOUVER

ONLINE **DANGER**

HOW TO PROTECT YOURSELF AND YOUR LOVED ONES FROM THE EVIL SIDE OF THE INTERNET

Published in New York, New York, by Morgan James Publishing. Morgan James is a trademark of Morgan James, LLC. www.MorganJamesPublishing.com

The Morgan James Speakers Group can bring authors to your live event. For more information or to book an event visit The Morgan James Speakers Group at www.TheMorganJamesSpeakersGroup.com.

ISBN 9781683505334 paperback
ISBN 9781683505341 eBook
Library of Congress Control Number: 2017907388

Cover Design by:
Rachel Lopez
www.r2cdesign.com

Interior Design by:
Chris Treccani
www.3dogcreative.net

In an effort to support local communities, raise awareness and funds, Morgan James Publishing donates a percentage of all book sales for the life of each book to Habitat for Humanity Peninsula and Greater Williamsburg.

Get involved today! Visit
www.MorganJamesBuilds.com

*This book is dedicated to
all of the hard-working Law Enforcement Officers,
who work tirelessly to keep us safe from the dangers
that lurk in both the real world and cyberspace.*

ACKNOWLEDGMENTS

Two of the most exciting moments as an author are when you start a book and when you finish it. Between those two events falls a lot of work and amazing people who support you along the way. I truly believe that everyone stands on the shoulders of other people, who have helped and provided guidance to get you to your current state.

My story is no exception. From when I was young to where I am now, I want to thank all of the friends, families, and colleagues who believed in me, pushed me to be my best, and offered a word of encouragement when it was most needed.

Most important is my amazing family, who all support me with any endeavor I go after and provide a pat on the back if I am down or a kick in the pants if I am not operating at my full potential. And above all, they say "I love you, and I am proud of you" at the end of each day.

From a book perspective, starting from the beginning is my friend and colleague Ted Demopoulos, who introduced me to my publisher, Morgan James Publishing. Karen Anderson made me feel like family from the moment we met, and we hit it off on aligning and getting everything needed for the book. Thanks to David Hancock for a wonderful dinner in Nashville and an amazing evening of conversation. Tiffany Gibson jumped in and gave me the guidance and direction that was needed.

All I can say is I am a big believer in reading and replying to LinkedIn ads because it allowed me to meet an amazing group of people at ProResource. When I needed an editor, I went to the best. Judy Schramm, Jen Hitchcock, and Mona Neff are the dream team that helped turn my words into an amazing book. Jeff Haas jumped in like a pro and took care of the illustrations. As we wrap up the writing, I can say that this team made the book not only such an enjoyable experience, but made me sound like I know what I am talking about.

One of the things that I do not like about writing acknowledgments is that you always forget someone very obvious and very important. For that person, just remember that I love you, thank you, and please forgive me.

Finally a book means nothing without people to read it, so to everyone who picked up a copy of this book, thank you for being awesome.

CONTENTS

This entire book focuses on security and powerful knowledge to keep yourself, your family, and your company as safe as possible. Every chapter contains actionable steps that you can take to minimize your chance of compromise.

Our use of electronic devices has us living in a fully connected world in which almost every action leaves a digital trail. It's easy to focus on the new functionality, but we also need to consider the dangers that accompany technological advances. Tips on first steps to make your Internet experience secure.

The Internet did not create more evil people, but it allows more people to perpetrate evil faster and with less conscious thought. To be protected, we need to understand why the cyber world presents more dangerous challenges than the physical world. Tips on developing cyber sense and how to safely dispose of devices.

Chapter 3: Secrets and Lies

Cyberspace is a scary place, and you must be careful. One hundred percent security is impossible, but with awareness, common sense, and a few tricks, you can enjoy the benefits of cyberspace. Tips on developing awareness and avoiding scams.

Chapter 4: Losers, Slime Balls, Forlorn Lovers, and Predators

A reliable way to verify online identities does not exist. Before you accept a follower request, chat with a potential date, or start a conversation on a fan page, think twice. Who is really at the other end of your communications? Tips on thwarting viruses and other cyber attacks.

Chapter 5: You Are the Target

Large corporations and government agencies rank high as cyber targets, but adversaries stalk you and your family, too. Make sure your online habits don't improve their chances of success. Tips on creating strong (and memorable) passwords, guarding financial accounts, and more.

Chapter 6: Smile, You're Being Recorded! Permanently.

You'd be surprised how much of your life—location, photos, shopping, online browsing habits—can be viewed and tracked by other people. It's up to you to protect your digital footprints and fingerprints. Tips on using social media, backup, encryption, and cloud storage.

Chapter 7: Childproofing Cyberspace (for Kids and Adults!)

Kids need to be aware of the dangers of living in cyberspace and the consequences of careless postings. Teach your children about cyber safety, and you will protect yourself, too. Tips on proper social media etiquette and safety.

Chapter 8: Digital Convergence or Digital Divide?

From streaming movies to remote control houses, consumers and businesses must adjust to digital innovation. Cyber crime is moving at warp speed, too. Tips on staying secure as new technology moves off the desktop and into everyday activities.

Chapter 9: Is It Time to Become Amish?

If you have a job, pay taxes, or see a doctor, your personally identifiable information (PII) can be hacked. Tips to reduce your risk in cyberspace and minimize the impact of a compromise.

Chapter 10: Safety in a Digital World

While you cannot completely eliminate the risk of compromise, you can prepare a vigorous defense and timely response to attacks. Here's a road map with best practices for most online activities and behaviors.

INTRODUCTION

Now.

We want it now.

Our world so rapidly adapted to the possibilities of cyberspace, that not only do we want it all, but we also demand it now. Maybe information technology should be renamed instant technology.

No more watching a painfully slow download, waiting to talk to customer service during business hours, or checking a credit card balance when the snail mail arrives.

But do you ever feel like your trip on the information superhighway is a little too risky and you are not aware of the online dangers.

My journey into cyberspace began when I would take apart every household gadget I could lay my hands on, as soon as my mom turned her back. I have always wanted to know how technology works, and if I had to sacrifice an alarm clock or blender in the process, it has been well worth it.

This trip has taken me into the discreet world of intelligence, to corporate boardrooms around the globe. I work with policymakers and boards of directors. My interaction with the typical technology user is usually limited to my friends and family, who flood me with questions on topics from programming their DVR to installing antivirus software to quietly keeping track of their kids online.

That is actually what inspired me to write this book. Consumer cybersecurity is not very hard. Protecting your family and protecting yourself online does not require a degree in computer science. This book is filled with concrete advice and proactive tips aimed at making the digital world a safer place for all users.

I want to share with you my knowledge of cyberspace, so we can all enjoy the benefits of technology while minimizing the risks to our security that new technology creates.

Cyberspace is an extremely dangerous place, and everyone deserves to be safe when entering the digital realm. Be a warrior in cyberspace, channel your inner ninja.

And if you feel like technology is moving too fast, please make sure you have your children safely buckled in with a five-point harness!

You probably think I do not know much about parenting if I believe children have a hard time adapting to new technology. I do have three kids, and more than once I have seen them learn how to master a new app or solve a simple coding problem before I can even get my reading glasses on. But while children quickly pick up the "how" of technology, they often fall short when it comes to the "why." After all, they are kids.

Parents and educators not only need to stay abreast of new technology for themselves, but also so they can safely guide children through cyberspace.

Allowing kids to have smartphones, electronic devices, computers, and connectivity to the Internet with no oversight, structure, or discipline is a disaster waiting to happen. As adults, we need to set the example, explain what is right or wrong, and take away their devices if they act dangerously, or cruelly, online.

Cyberspace revolutionizes more than just the gadgets and computers in our lives. It also revolutionizes crime. Imagine giving the worst kind of criminals a host of superpowers: the ability to leap continents in a single millisecond, a cloak of invisibility, and unlimited resources. At the same time, law enforcement finds itself underfunded and hampered by a lack of strong legal protections both at home and abroad.

If you think the worst cyber crime that can ever happen to you is having your credit card number stolen, think again. Everyone thinks that bad things happen to other people—until something actually happens to them.

The sooner you realize you need a cybersecurity strategy, the more protected you will be. Everyone in cyberspace is a potential target.

I will let you in on a huge insider tip. If your cyber safety is compromised, there is an easy way to find the culprit.

Look in a mirror.

Now I have you either really confused or mad. If you are not an IT expert (and most people reading this book are not), you think it cannot possibly be your fault if a national retailer is breached, and cyber crooks make off with millions of credit card numbers.

Each of us is individually responsible for weighing the benefits of cyberspace against its many risks. If you bank online, determine if the convenience of automatic bill pay is worth the potential hassle of having money stolen from your account. If you find great joy in sharing personal achievements with friends and family on social media, think about the potential consequences of your posts falling into the wrong hands.

A responsible digital citizen holds himself or herself accountable for personal cyber safety. Which brings us to another point. Sometimes people make really bad decisions online. Like galactically bad. So when your boss finds out about a nasty comment you made about him via social media, do not try to blame confusing privacy settings. You shot yourself in the foot.

At this point, it would be a little hard for most of us to pull off of the cyber roadway. It just is not practical. And fortunately, it's not necessary. There are measures you can take to minimize risk and protect yourself, your family, and your business in cyberspace.

Like I mentioned, I serve as a resource for my loved ones when they need cybersecurity help. My children, my co-workers, my friends—they grant me the perspective to see that cybersecurity is more than numbers, more than a million credit cards breached or $1,000 stolen. Every record compromised, every account hacked is a person.

And I really care about their safety—and your safety. So join me as I show you how to drive safely in cyberspace, and maybe throw in a few ninja moves along the way.

CHAPTER 1

THE NEW WORLD ORDER

Do you spend more money on coffee and treats at Starbucks than you do on cybersecurity? In the grand scheme of things, which one is more important? When it comes to your and your family's cybersecurity, do you opt for a skinny latte or a double shot of espresso?

In a world that is changing at a pace never before seen in our history, astonishing advances in technology play out before our eyes. With the advent of personal electronics, I often wonder, how did we ever survive without cell phones, tablets, and computers? How did we occupy our days, nights, and weekends?

My teenagers spend most of their time in front of a device, communicating with their friends. And hell hath no fury like a teenager grounded from cell phone privileges. When you take away electronic devices from teenagers or children, it is as if you are taking away their identity and, in fact, their very existence. Today's kids have no idea what to do, or in a scarier sense, how to operate without their electronics.

Whether we realize it or not, and most often kids do not, these devices have us living in a fully connected world in which almost every action we take leaves behind a digital fingerprint. It is easy for us to focus on all the new and enhanced functionality in our interconnected world, but we also need to consider the new dangers that accompany the technological advances.

Behind every email, every website, every packet that your computer receives, lurks the possibility of a malicious code with the potential to rock your world. Embarrassment, legal implications, financial loss, and even your identity are at stake. There is a new world order, and if you are not prepared, you can wind up on the short end of the stick, the victim of cyber criminal activity.

Organizations in Russia, China, and other locations work 24/7/365 to steal and exploit your digital information. The only question you have to ask: do you want to be a target? If you are not actively addressing online security, your default answer to that question is YES.

Most of us have done little to protect ourselves in a digital world. From experience, I can tell you that the cyber adversary plays a very effective offense. If you're not prepared to respond—or even better— to counter with a comparable effective defense, you are going to lose, and the losses can be significant. This book will teach you the tips and tricks of a vigorous cyber defense.

PERCEPTION OF SECURITY

When I meet people at parties or airports, and they ask what I do, I tell them that I work in cybersecurity. Many people exclaim that it must be the coolest job. But people's responses have not always been so positive. Fifteen years ago, that same career conversation garnered me some weird looks, like I was the smelly kid on the school bus.

Old-school thinking was that cybersecurity existed only for governments with classified information and for large companies with proprietary secrets to protect. Today, everyone—every single individual of any age—needs cybersecurity, and I consider myself blessed to work in an industry that is helping to make the world a safer place.

If you are not convinced that everyone needs cybersecurity, please turn on the television or pick up a newspaper and read the most recent—and the ongoing—reports about cybersecurity breaches. No company or government is immune to today's cyber adversaries; it seems that every aspect of commerce or communication, government or global entity can be compromised. And, are you ready for the scariest information of all? Most breaches pass undetected or unreported, so what you see or read about reflects only a small piece of the problem.

Those of us who work in cybersecurity call this perception the "iceberg effect." What you can see of an iceberg above the waterline represents a small percentage of the overall problem because most of an iceberg hides underwater, invisible and dangerous. The state of cybersecurity looks bad, but like the looming iceberg, the problem is a lot worse than most people realize.

Despite more than twenty years of rapid technological change, the average person only recently began recognizing cybersecurity as a problem to be addressed. The dangers in online interactions have always existed, but the problems are just now unfolding as an epidemic. No matter your age, background, or location in the world, if you use electronic devices, you must be vigilant about cybersecurity, and this book is written for you.

FALSE PERCEPTIONS MAKE YOU A TARGET

Leaked photos from a celebrity smartphone. A presidential candidate's leaked emails. Embarrassing voicemail messages left by a future king. Only celebrities get hacked, right?

WRONG.

Just like celebrities, you own a bank account, carry a credit card, and fill out online shopping forms—creating digital data in a wide variety of other ways. That personally identifiable information, or PII, forms your electronic identity. PII is priceless, regardless to whom it belongs.

Cybersecurity lingo includes the word "harvesting." Think of the cyber adversary as a farmer. Cyber crime is a risky business, and not every seed will sprout into a profit-yielding crop. But, just like in legitimate farming, a bigger harvest usually equals a better profit.

A massive field might be too much for one farmer to handle, and the same holds true for the cyber criminal. Breaking the harvest into smaller parts, and different plants, makes for an easier yield. This strategy, too, works for the hackers.

To be more specific, breaking into one large organization to steal 5,000,000 records works for cyber thieves, but larger companies can deploy tough defenses. On the other hand, most individuals have little-to-no security protecting their online identities and assets, making it much easier for hackers to break into 5,000,000 individual computers to steal personally identifiable information. The net effect remains the same: big profit for cyber criminals and big losses for their victims.

Cyber adversaries also favor so-called "watering hole attacks." Hackers target large sites accessed daily by millions of people, infiltrating cyber defenses for short periods of time. Even when the compromise of a major site lasts for just sixty minutes, it will net a significant harvest for the cyber thieves.

Wherever you go in cyberspace, and whoever you are, evil exists, and you need to be prepared.

And, instead of getting better and safer, the dangers and challenges of cyber defenses multiply every day.

Twenty years ago, I worked a compromise of 10,000 stolen records (i.e. credit cards, personal information), which was considered a large-scale incident. I told a friend that if we ever got to the point when 100,000 records could be stolen, that would signal trouble.

A few years later, working a case with 100,000 stolen records, I insisted that a million stolen records would signal that the situation was out of control. Just a few years later, we reached that million-records breached mark. Still, I would not give up. I contended that tens of millions of records stolen would result in chaos. Sure enough, a few years later it happened, and today we're edging towards a billion stolen records as the new norm.

It might be easy to blame third parties—banks, retail stores, the government—for not protecting your information. Certainly, those institutions and companies should be held accountable. But ultimately, each one of us, each individual, must accept responsibility for keeping our personally identifiable information properly protected.

The bottom line: when your identity and personal information are compromised, you are the one left to deal with the repercussions. Not the credit bureau, the retailer, or the government agency—though they may take steps to support your recovery. Nonetheless, if you want to win in cyberspace, YOU must take responsibility for your own protection and implement security today.

DEFENSE IN DEPTH

No single solution can make you 100 percent secure. That lack of absolute protection fuels a billion-dollar cybersecurity industry, where cyber breaches dominate consumer news.

Long ago, I coined a key phrase, "Prevention is ideal, but detection is a must." Truly, you will not be able to stop all attacks, but you should make it your goal to minimize or control the damage. You can start by implementing a variety of defenses, such as endpoint security, but you must also recognize those measures—all of them— can be bypassed by expert cyber criminals. You must always be alert for signs of an attack. When you notice unusual activity, do not ignore it; take immediate action.

Traveling through an airport, you often see signs imploring, "If you see something, say something." The same philosophy holds for personal protection. If you see strange activity, call the bank or credit card company and investigate the questionable charges. The sooner you detect an intrusion and take action, the more you can control— and perhaps limit—the damage.

"Defense in depth" is another common term in the cyber industry, and the term means to deploy multiple defense measures to protect your system. Defense in depth is all about diversifying your portfolio.

Consider your 401k or other savings: No smart investor puts 100 percent, or even 90 percent, of their assets in one fund; that plan would be way too risky. Instead, investors diversify, so that if one fund fails, the other investments minimize the impact on the total portfolio.

When you think of security, you need to identify multiple levels of protection and never depend on a single mechanism to make you secure. Take a moment and think of the possible layers of physical security for your home: You might live in a gated community, have an alarm system installed, and own a large dog named Fido that roams the halls. You might also sleep with a pistol in your nightstand and possess the martial arts skills of a certified ninja. Think of cybersecurity in the same manner: Be a cyber ninja.

Can you think of at least three different measures that you have put in place to protect your personal information online? If you cannot, this book is for you.

If you can name three measures that you've implemented to protect your PII, continue reading because there is no such thing as too much security. The ultimate question is: how effective is your overall security?

No matter your answer, do not let yourself become complacent. Adversaries are very smart and constantly aggressive, and the moment that you take your online security for granted, you make their job easier.

SECURITY 101

This entire book focuses on security and powerful knowledge to keep you, your family, and your company as safe as possible. Every chapter contains actionable steps that you can take to minimize your chance of compromise. To start, let's look at four basic cybersecurity principles.

1. **Always run the latest version of any software you install**. This principle applies to all software, including a device's operating system. Most software vendors, especially Microsoft, constantly improve product security and add new levels of protection.

   For example, Microsoft made huge changes and increased security from Windows XP to Windows 10. If you are running Windows XP, and you connect to the Internet, your system is highly vulnerable and probably has been compromised. Outdated software is the greatest gift you can give the adversary. Keep reading to understand why.

2. **Do not put off installing patches from software vendors.** Bugs, vulnerabilities, or exposures constantly pop up in software. Vendors release fixes, or patches, to eliminate these problems. A patch is the vendor telling the world that a weakness exists in its software. Adversaries, who recognize that many people do not properly patch their systems, actively develop exploits and try to quickly break into the vulnerable software. The longer it takes you to patch, the greater the chance of compromise.

3. **Uninstall any software that you do not use.** Software programs, especially unused and outdated ones, create opportunities for adversaries. Think of each software program like a window in a house. The more windows in a house, the more opportunities an adversary has to break in. It only takes one unlocked window for your house to be vulnerable to a robbery.

   A computer is like a house. The more software programs installed, the more points of potential exposure an adversary can try to exploit to break in. Install and use as much software as you need, but get rid of any programs that go unused or are replaced by new or different ones.

4. **Never login using an administrator account for daily activity; always login as a normal user with limited access or privileges.** An administrator can do anything on a system and can bypass most of the security controls. When (notice I use the word "when," instead of "if") your account gets compromised, the adversary will have the same level of system access you have. If the administrator account gets compromised, the

adversary gains total access to everything on your system. On the other hand, if an adversary gains access to your system as a simple "user," there will be some information that cannot be compromised.

You always want to operate with the least amount of privileges. Follow the golden rule of "never, ever surf the web or check email as administrator." Surfing the web as an administrator is like driving a motorcycle without wearing a helmet. You might not get into an accident today, but it is a very risky thing to do. Do not take chances when it comes to your personal protection.

THE TWO MOST DANGEROUS APPLICATIONS

In fact, can you name the two most dangerous applications on planet Earth? What programs have caused more harm, more damage, more identity theft, and more monetary damage than any other applications? Nope, it's not Angry Birds or Candy Crush. The answer: email clients and web browsers.

Yes, email and web browsers are the conduits of most evil and are the tools of choice for the adversary to cause harm. More specifically, the harm and damage lie in opening email attachments and clicking on links to illicit websites.

Many people do not realize that email is not an authenticated method of communication. The source address listed has little to do with who the email came actually from. This information can easily be spoofed, and your mail server does nothing to authenticate the origin of the email. Even though an email might look like it came from a trusted source, do not believe it.

The good news is that receiving a standard email typically does not cause harm directly. Instead, the danger lies in opening an attachment that allows a system to be infected. In fact, users are their own worst enemy, as they are tricked into actions that ultimately cause harm to themselves.

A wide variety of trusted online repositories, like Dropbox, offer a much better way to transfer documents. These sites require both parties to authenticate their identities in order to upload or download documents.

While there is a wide range of attacks that can be done via the web, security advice can be reduced to, "Be careful what links you click on." Adversaries like to send a link (via email) that looks legitimate but when you click it, malicious code activates that can compromise your system or steal your credentials. For any site that you visit on a regular basis, it is much safer to bookmark it rather than click on an embedded link.

I will cover this in more depth later, but here is one of the most critical pieces of advice I can offer: do not click on attachments or web links unless you are 300 percent sure they are legitimate. And here's more essential advice: Never, ever click on a link that looks like it came from your bank or the IRS. If you implement only these two practices, you will be saved a lot of money and heartache.

BUT I HAVE ANTIVIRUS SOFTWARE

After I speak at conferences, people often tell me that they feel safe because they have endpoint security or antivirus software installed on their systems. While a very important thing, installing these programs does not give you permission to be careless—or foolish. Endpoint security and web-filtering programs minimize common types of attacks, but more advanced malware can bypass these mechanisms and infect your system.

To return to our car analogy, wearing a seat belt in a car is a good idea, but it does not mean that you will not get into an accident or get hurt. Even when you wear a seatbelt, you still should be very careful when you are driving. Navigating the complex world of cyberspace is no different: even when you have antivirus software, you need to be careful.

Additionally, remember that adversaries are very clever and very smart—they do not like to get caught. Therefore, they constantly look for ways to get around antivirus and endpoint security protection. The game, often referred to as "attacker leap frog," works like this:

+ The bad guys constantly look for ways to bypass current security measures and compromise your system.
+ When the adversary is successful, the cyber defenders at security software companies actively work to figure out ways to defend against these attacks and stop the adversary.
+ When the cyber good guys successfully stop the attacks, the adversary figures out a different way to bypass the software. And, the game continues indefinitely.

So, in addition to installing these measures, you must also keep your antivirus and endpoint security software up to date. Do not let the annual license costs deter you—these programs play an important role in cybersecurity.

WHO IS TARGETING YOU?

Slime balls.

Scum of the earth.

Just as immoral and unethical people populate our physical world, they also exist in cyberspace.

My blood still boils when I think of a particularly nasty cyber attack that targeted widows of police and firefighters after the terrorist attacks of September 11, 2001. An email circulated, which appeared to offer help to those families with their loss and to handle compensation benefits for free. In reality, the adversary gathered PII, accessed bank accounts, and wiped out the savings of many survivors.

Essentially, the slime balls stole the financial security of many defenseless people and targeted people who had just lost their loved ones. If people who behave like that are not the definition of the scum of the earth, I do not know who or what is.

We all face similar types of danger in the cyber world. Adversaries will strike when you are most vulnerable; they search for those weaknesses and exploit them as opportunities. Be suspicious. This is not to say you have to be miserable, but truly, trust no one.

CONSIDER YOUR CHILDREN

Kids have not been exposed to evil, and therefore they do not understand or anticipate it, especially in cyberspace. That naiveté can lead to unwise social media choices and relationships. Over several months, the predator builds a relationship with your child, and at some point, the slime ball will ask for your child's address or will discover where the child attends school. The cyber stalking now gets real by becoming physical stalking, and the predator either approaches and/ or abducts the child. I wish this scenario was a one-off case, but it happens a lot more times than you would believe.

I know that some readers do not want to accept that such horrible things could happen, or worse, that you could unwittingly play a part in it. Those readers will dismiss this section. Or perhaps as a defense mechanism against the overwhelming evil of such situations, some readers will try to convince themselves that this kind of scenario is simply not true, but rather it is the result of Internet myths. Either way, denying the potential evil and harm that exists in cyberspace is a very unwise thing to do.

The golden rule of being safe online is that anything you say and do, can and will be used against you by slime balls. One of the main goals of this book is to offer new, real-world perspective and to re-train people's brains and behaviors to respond to what's really happening online.

For readers in denial: Please, you need to accept that the way you currently see the world is naïve and incorrect. Based on this newfound insight, you must continually ask yourself, "What do I gain and what do I lose by performing these actions?" It is also a good idea to always ask, "How could this information be used to target me or my family?" You absolutely must start to change your activity.

SURVIVAL OF THE FITTEST

Two general types of attacks exist in cyberspace: opportunistic attacks and targeted attacks. Most attacks, with monetary impact and negative outcomes, are opportunistic attacks that can be avoided. Opportunistic attacks target a large population, recognizing that only five percent of the targeted group will become actual victims—but five percent of 10,000,000 is a significant number.

The good news? You do not have to be in that five percent of victims.

On the other hand, targeted attacks are specifically aimed at an individual or entity, and they are often the work of a foreign government or organized crime. I will be honest: if you are the sole target of a cyber attack, you have bigger problems than the state of your cybersecurity. You need more help than this book can provide.

Fortunately—or not—targeted assaults typically focus on large organizations with significant amounts of valuable information. If you follow the tips and tactics in this book, you should be able to avoid, or at least minimize, the potential of ever being the focus of a targeted attack.

And, with that in mind, we will concentrate on implementing protection against opportunistic attacks.

If you are alive, which I am assuming you are since you are reading this book, you already know something about how to survive.

Like in nature, cybersecurity bases itself on survival of the fittest. If you do not adapt, you do not survive. A key component of survival is common sense. Common sense tells you not to stick a fork in an electrical socket or to open the door to a stranger at two o'clock in the morning.

Most people acquire and build a strong, robust set of intelligence that enables them to make good choices and avoid bad decisions. The key to a safe and happy life: do not do stupid things. If you apply those very same principles to cyberspace, you will win and the adversary will lose. Summarizing this entire book in one phrase: remember, everyone on the Internet could be out to get you, use your common sense.

For some puzzling reason, when many people connect to the Internet, they act as if all common sense goes out the window. Because of this mindset, the amount of stupidity that occurs in cyberspace is mind-boggling. If people behaved in the real world the way they do in cyberspace, the population of planet Earth would be significantly less.

The Internet is a completely open, untrusted network. Most forms of online communication contain little-to-no built-in authentication, which would verify a degree of safety. Spoofing, or impersonating, another individual is simple and effortless to perform with online communications.

Let's take social media for example. Go ahead, pick one of your favorite social media platforms and ask yourself a simple question: when I setup my account, what did they require to authenticate or prove that I am actually who I claim to be? The answer: absolutely nothing. Anyone can set up almost any account without verification. Yet most people accept social media accounts at face value and believe those accounts to be authenticated and verified.

INSTANT CYBERSECURITY

Are you intimidated by—or wishing you possessed—the skills of elite cybersecurity specialists? Let me quickly introduce you to one of their most powerful strategies: Limit the external exposure of your system and devices.

When you buy a brand new computer, unpack it, and turn it on, the computer most likely exists in a secure state. (Sure, as you see in spy movies, shrink-wrapped software can be infected with malware, but it usually happens on specialized devices and is discovered quickly.)

If you use that computer in its isolated state—never connect it to the Internet, never install any software—it will stay in a secure state. External contact causes infections and exposes personal information. The most common external source of contact is the Internet, closely followed by external devices like USB devices or storage devices. If you can control those two items and carefully monitor any external software introduced to your computer, you have essentially mastered the tools of the elite.

MAJOR COMPROMISE VERSUS MINOR COMPROMISE

The idea of abstaining from all Internet connection is enough to make the average person's head explode. How would we get anything done?

While not practical for everyone, I will share one easy and effective solution for your personal devices.

First, ask yourself what a major cyber compromise versus a minor cyber compromise would look like in your life. What is the difference between a computer infection that leaks personal information compared to an annoying yet minor virus? The personal value you attach to your data determines the gravity of the compromise.

Cybersecurity and cyber hygiene come down to a simple principle: protect your data. The best method, if you can afford it, starts with owning two computers or personal devices.

Use one device for all of your personal information: taxes, bank

 accounts, passwords, and more. Use that device ONLY for those purposes. If you bank online, connect to the Internet and only go to the bank site, nothing else. When you are done, disconnect from the Internet—no email, no web surfing.

The other device should NEVER contain sensitive or personal information. Use it only for email and web surfing. If this electronic gets compromised, the impact is minimal because all of your high-risk data resides on a separate drive—on the other, secure-use-only device. If you can swing that second device, you can sit back, smile, and say "I got this." Who knew that cybersecurity was so easy?

WHY IS THIS HAPPENING?

When I attend cybersecurity conferences or deliver corporate keynote addresses, I am often asked, "With all of the security software and technologies available, why does cyber crime continue to grow?"

It is true. Even with the vast sums invested in security, and an increasing focus on embedding security into software, the problem seems to be getting worse, not better. There are many reasons for this.

First, just like in the physical world, dangers exist all around us, and we have learned to operate in a manner that minimizes our exposures to those threats. In the real world, we have history, experience, and an extensive knowledge base of how to operate to avoid getting hurt. The problem is, in cyberspace, we have a very short history, few experiences, and a small or non-existent knowledge base.

Many of us are the first generation exposed to cyberspace, and therefore, we have little to no knowledge to pass on to our children. In fact, in many cases, our children are smarter and more efficient on technology than we are, but because they are also naïve about the dangers in the world, they often become targets of cyber stalking, cyber bullying, and other cyber crimes.

Second, sophisticated adversaries constantly adapt and change how they compromise systems. Each time the good guys introduce new security measures, the bad guys identify weaknesses and develop ways to bypass increased controls.

FUNCTIONALITY LEADS AND SECURITY FOLLOWS

A third reason for the continued growth of cyber crime reflects the very powerful concept, which is worth understanding in any area of our lives, that functionality leads and security follows.

When new technology emerges, vendors and users focus on functionality, and in general, they either do not consider security or view it as an unneeded expense. They have a mentality of, "Look what we can do now!" versus one of "How can this open new doors to harm?" Or, "How can this great new product be used against us?"

As time passes and people engage with the product, users begin to understand the potential—or actual—dangers, and then, people become willing to pay for security and solutions. Of course, the problem with this approach is that people have to be negatively impacted before vendors implement change. We are reaching that point in cyberspace.

We see this progression in the auto industry. When first manufactured, cars did not have seatbelts, airbags, or anti-lock brakes. Only after people started suffering harm did we realize that cars needed these safety features. I remember when the seatbelt law passed in New York in 1984. People were freaking out—they actually used bolt cutters to remove seatbelts, as a form of protest.

Today, that mentality seems galactically stupid. A seatbelt serves to help you and increase your security, but people hate change. I am assuming that since you are reading this book, you want to change. When you read the advice I give, do not fight it, but instead, embrace it and recognize that it is meant to help you.

Like cars and other innovations, computers, electronics and software were built with an eye on functionality and life-enhancing features; security developed as a response to problems discovered in usage. And, truth be told, many vendors are reluctant to change their focus to include more security features. Software companies that make operating systems want to make money. Those companies make money by making customers happy. Customers are happy when things work. Customers are angry when things do not work.

Facing those basic demands, manufacturers believe they are left with two options. Option one, turn on all functionality and turn off security, so everything works out of the box, and everyone stays happy (well at least initially, until they get compromised).

Option two, turn all connected functionality off, properly securing the application, but nothing works, and customers get angry. The second solution will cost software companies less money in the long run, with fewer patches and fixes. Just talk to an identity theft victim and ask them how much of their time a compromise cost them. They will quickly agree option two is better in the long run.

Unfortunately, the short-term drives most decisions, and option one wins. Do not feel hopeless. Most software today contains embedded, or built-in, security with features you can maximize. However, remember that while most computers, most operating systems, and most applications hold the potential to be secure, that security usually does not exist in the default state.

Don't leave your personal security entirely in the hands of someone else. Whenever you use any technology keep telling yourself, "This is not secure, and it can hurt me if I am not careful." The more you think about the negative consequences, the more protected you will be, and the smarter the decisions you will make.

CYBERSECURITY CAN BE AS PAINFUL AS PARENTING. THAT SAYS A LOT.

Quite honestly, a lot of security products miss the mark and neglect the root causes of cyber risk. Some applications do good things, but focus on the wrong things.

In fact, when I work with CEOs after major cybersecurity breaches, I often think of situations that parents encounter.

This year, when my son started high school, he came home the second week of classes and asked for my help. He said, "Dad, I just found that we are having a surprise quiz tomorrow, and I was wondering if you could help me study?"

Being the supportive dad, I said yes, but I was confused. Unless they changed the definition of "surprise," how did he know he was having a surprise quiz?

I asked him, with some hesitancy, how he knew about this alleged, surprise quiz. To be totally honest, I was cautious because like his dad, my son knows quite a bit about cybersecurity. Did he hack the teacher's computer? Being a security professional, I feared I faced a moral dilemma. If he broke into the system, should I high-five him for being clever or should I punish him for hacking?

Fortunately, the answer did not lie in cyber crime (whew), so I did not have to resolve that inner conflict. Apparently, the teacher told the students about a planned quiz on a surprise TOPIC.

I asked my son which subjects the teacher emphasized. He thought for a moment and answered mathematics. So we studied math. I gave him sample problems, and he got them all wrong. We worked together for three hours before it finally clicked. The next day he woke up for school confident and ready to take the surprise quiz.

I happened to be working from home that day, and I greeted him at the door when he arrived home. With a big smile I asked about the surprise quiz.

With his head hung low, he said it was rough. I tried to be encouraging—he knew that math inside out! "Dad," he said, "the quiz was on history. I wasted three hours studying when I could have been doing something much more useful like playing video games." (You have to love the mind of a sixteen-year-old and what he thinks is important.)

Undaunted, I tried to explain to him that the time he spent studying mathematics was still a good investment of his time, regardless of the surprise quiz and his score on it. He is going to need that math knowledge not only in high school but also in college. I am not sure he agreed.

This conversation is very similar to the ones I have at a corporate level. Organizations spend millions of dollars on security, and still, their systems get compromised. Despite best intentions, it can be impossible to know exactly how that "surprise" cyber attack will surface.

I walk into offices after a breach and the CEOs have their heads down. After a big sigh, they assert that the millions of dollars spent on security were wasted because systems were compromised anyway. As with my son, I explain that, without the investment, the damage would have been worse. The protocols deployed laid a solid foundation; however, in terms of stopping the adversary, it was not the right thing to do, and that is the fundamental problem.

You might be asking, what is the right thing to do when it comes to personal security? I refuse to leave you in too much suspense: protect and minimize the exposure of your sensitive information. The more you protect your critical information, the less overall damage an adversary can cause.

Some simple questions you should frequently ask yourself:

✦ What is my critical information or data that would cause harm if exposed?
✦ Where does that information or data exist?
✦ How can I better control or manage it?

As you think about and protect your data, you become a more and more unattractive target for an adversary.

READY, SET, GO!

Our new, interconnected world order presents boundless opportunities. But the same tools and technology present themselves to adversaries. In cyberspace, much as in the real world, anything that can be used for good can also be used for evil purposes. On the other hand, as long as we remind ourselves every day that we can become a target, and if we think before we click, we can reduce the harm that awaits us on the next website.

We CAN protect ourselves, our families, our companies, and the world we live in. The same skills that allow us to survive in the real world will protect us in cyberspace.

Here is what you need to remember to earn your cybersecurity black belt:

✦ The potential payday in cyber crime is enormous, so attacks will only worsen. As soon as investigators shut down one method of attack, adversaries adapt and find new techniques.

✦ Cybersecurity is often an afterthought. Designers first build devices that work well, and then consider security. Safety measures are often restrictive, so in the struggle between security and functionality, an efficient device comes out ahead.

✦ When your most commonly used programs issue new versions, upgrade. Instead of pinching cyber pennies, invest in improved software that is often more secure than older versions.

✦ Do not ignore those update reminders. When patches and updates to current versions of software are released, it usually is in reaction to known problems. Do not leave your systems vulnerable.

✦ When spring cleaning, do some cyber scrubbing, too. Uninstall all unused programs and eliminate potential problems.

✦ Always be yourself, and never be the administrator. Limiting use of the administrator account limits opportunities for major disaster if a system is breached.

✦ Email clients and web browsers are the two most dangerous applications in cyberspace. Email was never designed to be secure, and web links are vehicles for serious cyber attacks.

✦ Antivirus software is an important cybersecurity tool, but it should not be your only one. Adversaries work to circumvent the safety measures in software protections. Keep your antivirus software current and supplement your cybersecurity with some of the other tools and strategies I will introduce in later chapters.

✦ As dangerous as cyberspace is for you, the potential dangers for children are even greater. Never let go of a child's hand in this digital world.

CHAPTER 2

THE REALITIES OF CYBERSPACE

simple cipher with just two letters forms the basis of modern man's most complex inventions. Binary code built cyberspace. Without it, humankind would remain earthbound.

Whether we like it or not, our world runs on 1s and 0s, known as binary data; the digital code electronics use to communicate and store information.

While a little frightening, if those 1s and 0s cease to exist, most of our infrastructure would quickly stop working. Imagine a world without electronic devices, digital communication, and, gasp—no Internet!

Before nightmares about Arnold Schwarzenegger in *The Terminator* set in, let me assure you of the big difference between the words "run by" and "controlled by." Humans still control the world, and ultimately make critical decisions. Those decisions are often executed, or run, by a computer. Just like accepting a calendar invitation for a weekly meeting or the PTA bake sale, you decide whether or not you want to attend, and the computer takes care of the scheduling.

The difference between "run" versus "control" dominates the debate over self-driving cars. These cars ostensibly drive themselves, but ultimately humans create the logic used by these devices. Humans. Not the futuristic cyborgs Arnie battles in his hit movie series.

Humans are not perfect. That is what makes the world such an exciting place. Instead of getting mad the next time someone does something incomprehensible, embrace the fact that imperfection can make life exciting and can lead to new discoveries.

While imperfection can result in uniqueness, it can also lead to danger. Like the development of self-driving cars: given the imperfect nature of human achievement, programming flaws are inevitable. None of us will want to be on the highway the day self-driving cars are compromised.

Computers, networks, the Internet, cyberspace, and the digital world are human creations with human vulnerabilities susceptible to exploitation. The potential for evil runs rampant in our world, and perhaps even more so in cyberspace.

The Internet did not create more evil people; it just allows more people to perpetrate evil faster and with less conscious thought. Cyber adversaries tap into their dark side because the anonymity of cyberspace acts as a shield. Without a face to put with a target, many criminals view cyber attacks as victimless crimes.

WHERE'S THE HISTORY?

To be protected in cyberspace, we need to understand why, in many cases, the cyber world presents more dangerous challenges than the physical world.

Villains walked the earth as cavemen. Today, urban dwellers quickly learn the safer areas from the, well, not-so-safe neighborhoods. Running on a sidewalk in the park during the day is safer than running through the woods at midnight. This is common sense, and historic knowledge developed through trial and error.

Hackers do not have such a far-reaching history. Cyberspace is in its infancy, and we have little institutional knowledge about the how and why of what people do in cyberspace, both good and bad.

People born in 1993 and later are the first generation exposed to the digital revolution for their entire lives. Folks born earlier—parents, teachers, and business people—use technology as a means to connect, communicate, and transact business, but they do not have full immersion experience and knowledge from birth.

Meanwhile, in most areas of our lives, progress and technology lead, and security follows. People do not see the need for security until we learn and understand the risks of new technology. That paradigm, like most paradigms, resists change. Foremost consideration focuses on short-term gain, not on long-term consequences.

When online banking took off around the turn of the century, people asked why I resisted its convenience. Even after a quick tutorial on digital security dangers, most folks thought I was crazy. They failed to understand that online banking creates new criminal targets, with the bull's-eye directly on the backs of consumers.

For the record, people still look at me like I am crazy today; some things never change.

But when you let your guard down, the potential for people to commit stupid human tricks increases exponentially.

EVIL LURKS IN CYBERSPACE

The average consumer does not understand how cyberspace works. If you do not understand how something operates, you will not be able to identify possible exposure points. Most people think the Internet is magic, and at many levels, it is pretty awesome.

The fact that we can transfer money, send an email, or access data from anyone in the world changes everything in terms of how we live. It also changes everything in terms of how we are attacked.

When I am called upon as an expert witness, I love the chance to teach and explain cyber concepts. It's humbling to explain technical concepts to judges and juries in ways that they can understand and use to make important decisions. The experience also serves a constant reminder that many people do not grasp an accurate understanding of technology.

When I sit on the witness stand, I gauge juror faces to determine when I start geeking out and losing my audience to techie speak. I reel myself in and concentrate on more consumer-friendly explanations. How can anyone deliver an accurate verdict, inside or outside of a courtroom, without understanding the subject matter? While the Internet is a fascinating topic, it is not well understood.

By the way, do not worry, if you keep reading this book, you will get all of the answers you need to remain safe in cyberspace. I am fairly sure no one will call you paranoid, but I cannot guarantee it.

NOW HIRING: CYBER CRIMINALS

Just about anyone can be a cyber criminal because the hackers in the black hats are not writing strict rulebooks or job descriptions.

Bank robbers wear masks. Car thieves peer through vehicle windows searching for valuables. A pickpocket looks for a distracted tourist in a crowd. Investigators, and potential victims, operate with knowledge about criminal profiles and suspicious activity. Law enforcement officials access large databases of known bad guys to track, arrest, and minimize the chances of criminal activity.

On the other hand, cyber profiles, databases, known perpetrators, and modus operandi change faster than anyone can keep track.

Did you know that you might unknowingly be a cyber criminal?

Something as seemingly minor as reading someone else's email or logging in with a co-worker's credentials constitutes cyber crime. I talk with friends and colleagues who swear they would never commit a crime, yet in the last six months, they performed several cyber offenses.

Your mindset—that you did not intend to cause harm or did not know an action was a crime—does not change the fact that you committed a crime. Ignorance of the law is not a valid plea.

In the fight against cyber crime, we lack a clear-cut definition of the adversary.

ADAPTABLE ATTACKERS

Criminals, especially cyber criminals, are flexible and resourceful, changing attack methods to bypass defensive measures. A bank only has so many doors. In comparison, computers, tablets, phones, and networks sit practically wide open. A cyber door slams shut with a new defense mechanism, and the adversaries build a new door. Hackers can access the same technology and defense deployed by cybersecurity specialists.

Compounding the problem? The majority of commercially sold and implemented security measures address the symptoms of cyber backdoors, not the root cause of an issue, leaving space for new kinds of attacks.

A MAP WITH NO BOUNDARIES

Cyberspace defies international boundaries. Beyond technological standards, the Internet lacks global standards of conduct, which is markedly different from the clear jurisdictions for prosecution typically present in the physical world. For example, if you commit a hands-on crime in Pismo Beach, California, Pismo's local laws, and maybe federal laws, govern the legal process and penalties.

On the Internet, an adversary in Russia might access servers in Great Britain to illegally enter a computer network in the United States.

So, what laws are broken? Who takes the lead in the investigation? No stealthy band of ninja soldiers patrols cyberspace. The Internet connects the world without connecting cyber laws. And that assumes law enforcement can even determine who committed the crime, a whole other challenge in cyberspace.

CYBERSECURITY AS AN AFTERTHOUGHT

Imagine your home. Building codes mandate safe, residential-construction standards. An inspector verifies that each phase of a project adheres to code. The end result: a safe dwelling that properly protects your family from hazardous housing violations.

Have you ever heard of a cyber inspector? Nope, the position does not exist. When a design team unveils a new digital product, no regulator stands by to ensure safety. Quite often, developers tack on security as an afterthought, following the rush to create and launch a financially successful technology.

A handful of U.S. regulations exist to safeguard personal, financial, and credit card data. However, focus is on disclosure penalties, and legal requirements generally lack mandatory security measures. Sporadic enforcement complicates matters.

The closest exception to these shortcomings is the Payment Card Industry Data Security Standard (PCI DSS).

PCI DSS defines security processes for any business handling or storing credit card information. But the financial industry, not regulators, created PCI DSS. Individual credit brands (VISA®, MasterCard®, American Express®, and others) govern enforcement, compliance, and penalties. Those corporations carry a big stick. However, many businesses, large and small, are still not compliant. PCI DSS defines security best practices and carries significant weight, but it is not the law.

SAME THREAT, DIFFERENT VENUE

Cyber adversaries are creative, yet they lack originality. Despite new and nefarious attack modes, most cyber threats mimic the crimes committed in the physical world: extortion, blackmailing, stalking, and bullying. Cyberspace facilitates and hastens crimes as old as time.

In the old-fashioned criminal world (which still thrives), bad guys actually venture out and locate a victim. Criminals expose themselves to danger and detection.

A cyber criminal hides behind a keyboard and leaves only a spotty trail of evidence. Cyber bullies send threatening texts from a mobile phone. Almost gone are the days of backing underclassmen up against the locker when a teacher turns his or her back. A bully now can harass victims halfway around the globe.

Because cyber criminals do not have to literally "face a victim," cyber crime will only continue to grow. One morning, as I took a break from writing this book, the television at the gym was turned to a local news report about death threats made via social media. Why, the reporter asked, is this happening? The expert replied, oftentimes people fail to see social media and email as "real." Adversaries feel protected behind their computers, without realizing their threats constitute a crime. Yup, that talking head nailed it.

PARANOIA IS YOUR FRIEND

A solitary ninja trusts no one. Neither should you.

While my family members will probably roll their eyes with this next piece of advice, I insist cyberspace requires a healthy dose of paranoia.

I offer you the same advice for driving on the information super highway that I provided to my son when he received his vehicular license. The advice is simple: every driver represents danger, and people will try to hurt you. Whether online or on the highway, you can never be too cautious. Sadly, many cyber victims are vulnerable, trusting, and commit mistakes they would be too savvy to make in the physical world.

TOO GOOD TO BE TRUE

Both good guys and bad guys benefit from technological innovations. Anything used for good can be warped by evil. Since most of us are not evil (thankfully), we find it hard to imagine that others deliberately try to hurt us.

The so-called Nigerian bank scam still catches the susceptible off guard. It looks something like this:

> Dear Sir, SEEKING YOUR IMMEDIATE ASSISTANCE.
> Please permit me to make your acquaintance in so informal a manner. This is necessitated by my urgent need to reach a dependable and trustworthy foreign partner. This request may seem strange and unsolicited but I will crave your indulgence and pray that you view it seriously. I am from the Democratic Republic of Congo and one of the close

aides to the former President of the Democratic Republic of Congo LAURENT KABILA of blessed memory, may his soul rest in peace.

Due to the military campaign of LAURENT KABILA to force out the rebels in my country, I and some of my colleagues were instructed by Late President Kabila to go abroad to purchase arms and ammunition worth of Twenty Million, Five Hundred Thousand United States Dollars only (US$20,500,000.00) to fight the rebel group. But when President Kabila was killed in a bloody shoot-out by one of his aide a day before we were schedule to travel out of Congo, We immediately decided to divert the fund into a private security company here in Congo for safe keeping. The security of the said amount is presently being threatened here following the arrest and seizure of properties of Col.Rasheidi Karesava (One of the aides to Laurent Kabila) a tribesman, and some other Military Personnel from our same tribe, by the new President of the Democratic Republic of Congo, the son of late President Laurent Kabila, Joseph Kabila.

In view of this, we need a reliable and trustworthy foreign partner who can assist us to move this money out of my country as the beneficiary. WE have sufficient "CONTACTS" to move the fund under Diplomatic Cover to a security company in the Europe in your name. This is to ensure that the Diplomatic Baggage is marked "CONFIDENTIAL" and it will not pass through normal custom/airport screening and clearance.

Our inability to move this money out of Congo all This while lies on our lack of trust on our supposed good friends (western countries) who suddenly became hostile to those of us who worked with the late President Kabila, immediately after his son took office. Though we have neither seen nor met each other, the information we gathered from an associate who has worked in your country has encouraged and convinced us that with your sincere assistance, this transaction will be properly handled with modesty and honesty to a huge success within two weeks.

The said money is a state fund and therefore requires a total confidentiality. Thus, if you are willing to assist us move this fund out of Congo, you can contact me through my email address above with your telephone, fax number and personal information to enable us discuss the modalities and what will be your share (percentage) for assisting us. I must use this opportunity and medium to implore You to exercise the utmost indulgence to keep this Matter extraordinarily confidential, Whatever your Decision, while I await your prompt response. NOTE: FOR CONFIDENTIALITY, I WILL ADVISE YOU REPLY ME ON MY ALTERNATIVE EMAIL BOX Thank you and God Bless. Best Regards

Sophisticated email users instantly delete messages like this. But this type of email continues to victimize millions of people, feeding off the get-rich-quick dream. It also takes advantage of another fact: consumers often fail to verify digital authenticity.

My dad owned a garden center on Long Island. Fighting off a tide of competitors, my dad always told me, and his customers, if it sounds too good to be true, it probably is. From fertilizer to shovels and email offers to shady websites, consumers throw common sense out the window in pursuit of the unbelievable deal or the quick buck.

Widespread education efforts rendered the Nigerian scam less effective, but the email still circulates because recipients still fall for it. Even small changes to the script increase the pool of potential victims, and adversaries can be clever and deceptive writers. When any type of attack no longer works, the adversary will stop sending it.

Email scams play off the numbers. Cyber crooks do not need a million people to respond. Every victim represents a potential profit. Many of those scammed quickly realize they fell for a hoax. Time and time again, friends and family members call me after they have done something silly in cyberspace and ask how to fix it.

Unfortunately, there is no time machine in cyberspace. So. Stop. Doing. Stupid. Things.

Assume every ping in your electronic mailbox is dangerous, and be very careful about what you do, what you open, what you post, and what you say in cyberspace.

THE MYTH OF 100 PERCENT SECURITY

One hundred percent security cannot be guaranteed in the cyber world. No matter how many safeguards you put in place, there will always be some risk.

Revisit a concept introduced in the first chapter: cyber functionality and 100 percent security are mutually exclusive. Disable all vulnerable features on a device, and you will achieve pretty close to 100 percent security. But when you do that, you are left with a worthless hunk of plastic, metal, and computer chips. The value of your system balances at zero.

If you enjoy the functionality and benefits of cyberspace, at some point you will suffer a compromise. But effective security can minimize the negative impact.

Life is risky. One morning you could slip and fall in the shower. You might get rear-ended driving to work. We attempt to mitigate dangers, but risk is always present. In the cyber world, as in the physical world, the aim is to keep risk at an acceptable level.

WHAT IS A TYPEWRITER?

My son and I ran across a typewriter as we cleaned out the basement. Frustration ensued as I tried to explain ink ribbons, while he looked for the typewriter's spell-check function.

This conversation got me thinking about the control we have lost in the digital world. If I used a typewriter to create a single copy of a document, shredding that paper destroyed all traces of the data it contained.

That luxury no longer exists. Every electronic move we make leaves behind a digital vapor. Documents can no longer be erased with high confidence. When you delete a document, you are not really deleting it. You are just telling the computer to forget where that document can be found. But cyber eggheads can recover a remarkable amount of erased and lost information.

CYBER AIRBAGS

I will say it again: functionality drives the digital world; security plays second fiddle. Harm or loss spur most security updates. Therefore, many of the technologies we rely on are not designed to be secure.

Inherent security, that is, security included as a priority when creating a digital product, should fuel digital design. But, as with safe cars loaded with security features, a computer is only as safe as the person navigating it.

Most people never formally learn how to drive on the information super highway, resulting in reckless behavior. All the airbags in the world cannot help those drivers.

Almost all valuable data in our lives will be, at some point, stored in digital format, immortalizing that information and opening it up to potential compromise.

Never give away or just throw out a computer when it becomes obsolete. Even if you delete your pictures, documents, and files, they remain hidden within the inner workings of your device.

Remove hard drives before recycling electronics, or use secure wiping techniques. Overwrite the hard drive. High-powered magnets, known as degaussers, permanently erase data stored on devices. Do not forget, almost all electronics, including tablets and cell phones, contain hard drives.

Always remember this simple advice: protect your devices, protect your data, protect your life.

READY, SET, GO!

Cyberspace offers many benefits, but also opens up an additional playground for the adversary. Most people only look at the benefits but fail to realize the inherent dangers. Once you understand the dangers, you can start to implement effective solutions to protect your personal and professional lives.

Here is what you need to remember to earn your cybersecurity black belt:

✦ Cyberspace is still a new frontier. Most users benefit from its advantages, without understanding how it works.

✦ Cyber criminals are relatively new, too. But they are very good at changing and adapting to new realities of cyberspace.

✦ Think twice before even trusting your mother in cyberspace. A little skepticism will not hurt you.

✦ Flawless security does not exist.

✦ Learn how to properly recycle electronic devices and permanently delete data.

CHAPTER 3:

SECRETS AND LIES

*E*ven the boldest adventurer feels a frisson of dread when facing *a new cyber galaxy. Do not be afraid to explore cyberspace. Here are the secrets and lies, revealed.*

FUD.

Fear. Uncertainty. Doubt.

Many people view cybersecurity with FUD. Instead of basing an opinion on half-truths and lies, allow me to explain the realities of cybersecurity and, perhaps, balance your thinking.

Yes, cyberspace is a scary place, and you do need to be careful. But with awareness, common sense, and a few tricks, you can still enjoy the benefits of cyberspace.

I often attend security talks where the speaker aims to frighten the pants off of listeners. While entertaining, scare tactics fail to provide much value. Listening to a convicted felon explain how he broke into systems gives you lots to talk about when you go to the bar with your buddies.

But without factual data and practical solutions, hype does little to protect you—especially if your system is already compromised or if you continue to repeat mistakes in how you navigate the Internet. The public deserves the plain truth about cybersecurity, coupled with actionable steps to shield our families, our organizations, our world, and ourselves.

Hacking is not magic. It requires preexisting conditions, or flaws, in a system. Experts often call cybersecurity a "zero sum game." No matter what you do, no matter how much money you spend, no matter how you configure your system, you will be compromised if an adversary sets his or her mind to it.

Does all this mean that security is a lost cause? No way. If you assert cybersecurity is useless, I will buy you a t-shirt that says, "I'm

with stupid" and an arrow pointing at your head. One hundred percent security is impossible, in anything. In cyberspace, users need to recognize that there are no guarantees, but exposure can be minimized.

Cybersecurity should mirror security in the physical world by focusing on reducing exposure, not eliminating it. Reducing exposure can be done; eliminating it totally is simply not possible.

CYBERSPACE SECRETS

Everyone loves a secret. Not only can a secret make you feel special, but the right secret can also give you an edge.

I am a big fan of keeping journals and notes. Every time I teach or deliver keynotes, I go back to my hotel room after the presentation, write down all the questions my audience asked, and how they reacted to different topics. Researching this chapter, I went back through many of my journals, digging out the biggest tips, tricks, and insider secrets to surviving in cyberspace. Shhh, here they are.

You are your biggest danger. There are two general types of threats: external and internal. External threats hit the news constantly—foreign governments, organized crime, rogue competitors, or whistleblowers. Yes, most cyber threats are initiated from the outside. But they are usually made possible by an accidental insider; an authorized user who is tricked or manipulated to do harm. Most of the time, the accidental insider is you.

Employ mindful security. Cybersecurity hygiene requires a conscious decision. As with exercise or diet, changing bad cyber habits can be very difficult. Compelling evidence or drastic consequences drive most change. I want to provide you with enough compelling evidence to revamp your cyber practices (and help you to avoid drastic consequences). I really do care about personal cybersecurity: please take action and do not become a victim.

Being secure is a journey, not a destination. Cyber adversaries will always adapt and change, so your security must also adapt and change. Defensive measures evolve. Focus on the root causes of problems, not the symptoms. For example, if your device becomes infected after opening a harmful file attachment, do not completely shut down email traffic. Instead, stop opening attachments from unknown sources.

Security is not hard. Think of cybersecurity as a state of mind. If you look at it through the eyes of the adversary, identify attractive targets, and remove them, you are in a secure state. The good news? I am going to walk you through how to do exactly that.

Limit access and control. Simplified to the most basic concepts, cyber safety depends on controlling your system and controlling your data. If you block malicious code, or your data resides on an unconnected device, the adversary fails. Hold tightly to your data.

CYBERSPACE LIES

Too many bad security decisions and disagreements are based on rumors or lies. Here are some of the top falsehoods about cybersecurity.

The Internet is secure. The Internet was built and designed for sharing, not security. When using the Internet, security is the user's responsibility. Software developed to increase security exists, like secure socket layer or transport layer security (SSL/TLS). This technology protects your information in transit but does not protect your system from being compromised.

If you bank online, have you noticed how the URL address starts with "https" instead of the usual "http"? That little "s" indicates encryption, which protects your data, so hackers who intercept the data cannot read it. But that tiny little letter cannot keep your entire system secure.

System security relies on the decisions you make, boiled down to three actions: what email attachments you open, what links you click, and what websites you visit.

100 percent security exists. False, false, false. Notice how I keep coming back to this point? Your job entails containing and controlling the amount of damage caused by an attack. The scenario is very similar to how we handle potential fires in buildings. Buildings have cement walls called firewalls, smoke detectors, and sprinkler systems—none of which are meant to prevent fires, but are all focused on controlling the amount of damage caused by a fire.

New devices are secure out of the box. No technology is secure in its default state. Vendors provide tools and capabilities, but it is your responsibility to turn on and implement those functions. Consumers—excited over a new gadget, computer, or technology—just want to turn it on and use it. They do not want to wait to properly secure devices.

You will not be a target. Look in the mirror and repeat ten times, "I am a target." Users focus too much on thinking that, unlike a large company, personal devices contain nothing hackers want. All personal data carries potential value. Limit, control, and protect critical data. Do not make it easy for an adversary. Once you implement any security measures, you decrease the odds of compromise. YOU ARE A TARGET. When you believe that, and take action, you are protected.

SECURITY IS ABOUT RISK

I often get asked to define security. Security manages, mitigates, and reduces the risk to critical assets. Whether we like it or not, security is all about risk and the potential to lose critical assets.

Risk is "what if." Look at every possible scenario and use that information to define an acceptable level of risk. If the current risk rises above an acceptable level, put reduction measures in place. This consciousness needs to become a routine part of cyber behavior.

Why do you drive your car when it is sunny but stay home during a snowstorm? You analyze the hazards of driving before you put the key in the ignition. Perform this same analysis in cyberspace. Open email attachments from trusted sources. Delete attachments from unfamiliar addresses. Define your risk threshold.

Determine your critical data assets, calculate harm, and implement protection. Maybe your fantasy football draft choices rank low on your priority list. The password to your bank account probably deserves a higher level of protection. Define, prioritize, and protect.

TO TRUST OR NOT TO TRUST

Humans want to believe in other humans. If someone comes up to you and says his name is Pete, and he is from Virginia, you will probably believe him. Until Pete drops his driver's license and you see he is really Carl from Wyoming. In the physical world, we tend to trust others until we have a reason not to. Of course, prudence demands caution, but overall, we want to trust.

In cyberspace, this premise no longer works. Your high-speed wireless connection does not provide a window into the soul of the user on the other end of your communication. Because verifying electronic information is next to impossible for the average user, it simply is not done. This is where that healthy dose of paranoia comes into play—question everything.

If you are struggling with this perspective, do a quick cost-benefit analysis. If you continue to trust everyone online via email and social media, what do you gain, and what do you lose?

WHO CAN SPOT THE FAKE?

When you receive a message from Eric Cole, how do you know Eric really sent you an email? From email to social media, no reliable form of authentication or verification exists to confirm cyber identities. Adversaries find it ridiculously easy to spoof, or impersonate, a sender's email address.

Think of spoofing like the return address on any letter or package you send via snail mail. You can write anything, and no one checks it. The same holds true with spoofing.

As you navigate cyberspace, do not confuse spoofing with phishing. The terms are related, but refer to different actions, and you need to protect yourself against both types of threats.

In spoofing, an email appears to come from an authorized entity, one that is familiar to you. For example, if an adversary sends you an email that looks like it came from your bank or the government, even though it came from the adversary, the addressed was spoofed.

Phishing, on the other hand, utilizes spoofing to pretend to come from a legitimate entity but with the intent of causing you to take some action that puts you, your data, or your computer at risk. That action, which will seem so innocuous but is really quite dangerous, can be as simple as clicking on what looks like a harmless link or as opening an attachment.

How do you defend against spoofing and phishing? You use "out-of-band" authentication. That is, you must verify the sender's identity through a different communication medium. For example, when you receive an email, think of the source address as merely a suggestion of who the sender might be. Stop before you open it, and spend less than a minute to confirm an email's legitimacy via a phone call, text, or even a separate email to the apparent sender.

The same analysis holds true for attachments. When you receive an unexpected email from a colleague with an attachment, think before you open it. What are the chances the attachment contains something you need? What are the odds the communication is a spoofed email poised to infect your system?

Can you live with the downside? If the answer is no, pick up the phone or text the colleague to verify the email's authenticity. A few seconds spent on assessment and verification can save you hours of time (and money) spent on recovering and repairing your system.

Here is a very radical idea. Delete everything in your inbox. If it contained anything important, believe me, those people will contact you again. Try it: delete everything. It feels liberating.

UNSOCIAL MEDIA

Authentication problems caused by email are dwarfed by the threats posed by social media. A quick look at any social media platform reveals that most people post way too much personal information online. From photos of the bean soup they just cooked to where they are on vacation to what time each week their child attends soccer practice—the details are online for all the world to see—and exploit.

Why do so many users inherently trust everything they see on social media? I suppose if I could crack that nut I would be a very wealthy man indeed.

If the evil people in the world united to create a way to cause the greatest harm to the greatest number of people, they could not have done a better job than creating social media platforms. I imagine social media trailblazers, sitting in dorm rooms and garages, brainstorming about new forms of communication. "Hey," they thought, "let's create a website where people will voluntarily post their deepest, darkest secrets, and they will do it for absolutely free!"

Let me emphasize, I am not trashing social media; I am criticizing how people *use* it.

Social media profiles require zero verification to validate a user is actually who they claim to be. Sites typically do require users to abide by rules and codes of conduct that prohibit fake accounts. But again, as with almost everything in cyberspace, enforcement is scarce.

You must begin to think—but do NOT act—like a mischievous hacker who might want to cause harm to someone. Harm to someone like you.

First, and I apologize in advance—but trust me, no one really cares about the bean soup you made for dinner tonight. Oh, by the way, when you posted that recipe, a hacker broke into your social media account. There goes your identity! What exactly did you gain?

Next time you make something new or delicious, tell your mom (or your best friends) about the wonderful dinner you prepared. Perhaps this is not as gratifying as seventeen likes and four shares, but your identity remains safe from online dangers.

Second, next time you share online, ask yourself two questions.

+ Am I comfortable sharing this with my friends?
+ Am I comfortable sharing this with strangers?

Because once you put information out into cyberspace, there is no way to guarantee it will stay private.

Social media users are often tempted by quizzes, surveys, or other entertainment-oriented applications that request access to account information. The fun and informational aspects of these applications draw people into thinking they are safe and that there is no harm in allowing access to the requested info.

But, you must always remember that when you provide access to your personal accounts, you surrender personally identifiable information (PII), and potentially, control over how that PII will be used. If you like to use online games and applications, set up separate, "skeleton" accounts that contain little personal information, and use those skeleton accounts to play. You never, ever want to give away access to your primary social media accounts.

I know social media is not going away, and I will even concede that despite all of its flaws, it provides value. But you must remember to post wisely. In everything you do online, start training your mind to perform some basic risk analysis.

PLEASEROBME.COM

The website www.PleaseRobMe.com raises awareness about oversharing information online. I promise it is a real site that educates social media users about the potential pitfalls of location-sharing services. There is nothing inherently wrong with "checking-in" with your friends. The problem arises when nefarious individuals use the information about your physical location—gathered from applications for check-ins, online reviews, or other messages—as a road map for crime (cyber and real world).

It seems innocuous, but when you post, "Yum, great slice of pizza

at Joe's!" or "Movie date night—at State Theatre," you are really telling criminals, "I am not at home right now. Go for it."

Vacation posts blow my mind—please, post photos when you get home, people! I had to restrain myself when an acquaintance checked-in on social media, "Getting on the airplane with my family for a much needed vacation." Most responses said they were jealous, or have fun! I sat on my hands, so I would not type, "You moron! You just told the world that your home is unoccupied."

I may have a friend or two who avoid discussing cyber safety with me. It can be hard when your buddy looks at your beach vacation and only sees burglars ransacking your home. That said, you should never broadcast that you will be away for a long period of time. Adversaries adore social media and the human tendency to overshare.

Change your thinking, save your life. The typical online visitor's naiveté is a major reason so much lawlessness rules in cyberspace. Do not blame the victim, just investigate and deploy safe online behaviors to the very best of your ability.

AN INSIDE JOB

Online platforms, social media, and devices offer security features and options that users can turn on. But in most cases, the settings are turned off by default to maximize the functionality of a site. Security, again, lies in the hands of the user.

What security software comes with many devices? What kind of third-party applications should you use? Here are the basics.

Software Updates. Software vulnerabilities are frequently discovered, and manufacturers issue updates to address them. You must keep software up-to-date, installing all updates and patches as soon as you receive them. When the vendor releases a patch, they are basically telling the world that a vulnerability exists in their software. The longer your software remains unpatched, the bigger the exposure to attack.

Antivirus Software. Malicious software reigns as the most common source of system compromise. So-called "malware" is software that is meant to cause harm or damage to a system, the most prevalent being computer viruses. Viruses attach to applications on your system, so when you run those programs, you also run the virus, which infects a system and causes harm. Antivirus software detects this type of malicious code and stops it from running.

Host-Based Intrusion Prevention. While viruses are nasty, there are other types of malicious code that harm systems. Host-based intrusion prevention software (HIPS) monitors the system, looks for malicious behavior, and blocks the culprit before it can cause significant damage.

Application Whitelisting. Any application that runs or executes on a system carries the potential to cause harm. While antivirus software and HIPS will look for malicious activity, application whitelisting can be another valuable security tool. With application whitelisting, administrators create approved lists of applications. Only those applications are allowed to run on the system, and only if they have not been modified. Since adversaries change software to infect systems, application whitelisting makes it very hard for the adversary to cause harm. This is a slightly more advanced technique and may not be applicable on home systems.

Full Disk Encryption (FDE) for laptops. If you travel with a laptop, you guard it from potential loss. While losing an electronic device can be frustrating and expensive, losing sensitive data can be the biggest consequence of all. Taxes or bank records can be used to electronically steal funds and your identity. Trade secrets may fall into the wrong hands. If your laptop contains vital information, you should install

FDE software, which converts all device data into a form that can be understood only by the person who has the authentication key to decrypt the encrypted data.

The last four protections are third-party security software, also known as endpoint security or total security protection. This software can be very helpful, but even with these valuable aids, the security of a system is only as good as the security of the operator.

Too often, I encounter people who view security as an inconvenience, a nuisance, or a waste of time. Isn't cybersecurity worth five, ten, or even fifteen minutes of your time? It should be, because should your identity ever be stolen, it can take 200 hours or more to mitigate the damage.

So do you want to spend a few minutes on cybersecurity today, or 200 hours in the future? Do not say anything, I know your answer.

Anytime you use a new electronic device, service, or application, you have a job. Research features and options, asking yourself these questions:

+ What risks and exposures does this item pose?
+ Are there security features I can use to minimize the downside?
+ Can I change my behavior (i.e., be careful about what I share) to minimize the exposure?
+ Can I accept the potential negative consequence associated with this device or application?

When you learn a new skill, an internal training must occur. It takes time for a new activity to develop muscle memory and become intuitive. Therefore you have to force the new behavior until it becomes spontaneous and natural. Force yourself to ask these questions—maybe even put a copy of them where you can always see it—until they become second nature to you.

In cybersecurity years, consumers are pre-teens, figuring out what is right or wrong, and learning how to make better decisions. My guess is most readers may have already made some poor decisions online. You may have been infected by malicious code, hacked, or had your identity stolen. For those of you in this category, the decision to change is easy.

Adversaries are not going to stop causing harm; we have to learn how to integrate cybersecurity into our lives. Start thinking correctly and you will be able to enjoy all of the benefits of cyberspace and minimize the overall risks.

READY, SET, GO!

What's the biggest secret the adversary does not want you to know?

You can control your own cyber destiny. By being aware, asking questions, researching authenticity, and deploying security protocols, you can protect yourself. If something does not look real or feel right, hit delete. Be suspicious of every email and every website you visit, and you can go a long way to being secure online.

Advice is cheap and easy; acting on it is hard. If you avoid an incident, you deserve all of the credit for taking the advice to heart and acting on it. Be on the winning team because—let's face it—losing stinks!

Here is what you need to remember to earn your cybersecurity black belt:

+ Your own actions pose the greatest danger to your cybersecurity.

+ Security is a decision. Form good habits by finding the methods that work best for you.
+ Safe cyber practices are not learned overnight. It will take time, but it is worth the effort.
+ Limit access to your systems, and limit access to your data.
+ Every trip to cyberspace should be accompanied by a risk assessment. Determine if the gain from exposing your data is worth the potential harm if that data is compromised.
+ Always remember that you are a target. You will be breached.
+ Be on the lookout for counterfeits and fakes. Spoofing and phishing techniques can make almost any email, link, or attachment seem real.
+ Update and patch software as a regular part of your cyber hygiene.
+ Antivirus software offers a strong measure of protection against malware, one of the most common types of cyber attacks.
+ Be aware of bad behavior with host-based intrusion-prevention software, which flags suspicious behavior on your network.
+ Use only what you know. Create approved lists of programs, a process called application whitelisting, and only run that software on your systems.
+ Encrypt sensitive information, especially on laptops, which are mobile and therefore more vulnerable to theft.

CHAPTER 4:

LOSERS, SLIME BALLS, FORLORN LOVERS, AND PREDATORS

he glow of the computer screen is the only light in the room, flickering gently over the face of your next-door neighbor's son. He dropped out of high school and has never held a full-time job. His rap sheet is longer than the list of successful rap songs he thinks he could have written. But when his fingers float over his keyboard, he grows six inches taller, fifty pounds lighter, and he drives a sports car.

The first rule of delivering keynotes: be entertaining. When I face audiences to deliver talks on cybersecurity, the listeners usually feel pretty blasé about online safety. Sharing stories about some of the real life criminals living in cyberspace, like that neighbor's son, usually elicits some good laughs and engages listeners.

But what does not make me laugh? It's the fact that a reliable way to verify online identities does not exist. So before you accept the next follower request, chat with a potential date, or strike up a conversation on a fan page, you must think twice. Who is really at the other end of your communications?

A cyber criminal does not control his or her physical genetics, but they can create cyber genetics, appearing online as a deceptively charming and attractive individual. As someone you might want to add as a "friend" or connection.

In cyberspace, the truth is, when you deny a friend request or ignore an email, that choice could very well keep you from harm. Please, do not think I am overly dramatic. Over the past thirty years, I have seen more terrible cybercrimes than you can imagine.

A paramour fudges the height on his dating profile, rounding it up by an inch or two, and modifies reality. A job hunter claims credit for a project that she did not manage. Many good people do not see harm in degrees of truth. But online, when do those degrees cross the line?

In some ways, the Internet serves as a massive playground for mischievous and deceitful folks. If you are not careful and aware, you are a ripe target. Peel back the layers, and reveal the evil side of the Internet.

My favorite proverb explores the hazards of another dangerous playground.

> *Every morning in Africa, a gazelle wakes up.*
> *It knows it must run faster than the fastest lion,*
> *or it will be killed. Every morning a lion wakes*
> *up. It knows it must outrun the slowest gazelle, or*
> *it will starve to death. It doesn't matter whether*

you are a lion or a gazelle: when the sun comes
up, you'd better be running.

—*Abe Gubegna*

Every wireless network you join, each link that you click, every download you save holds the possibility that someone out there is targeting you. Do you control your own security, or does the adversary?

THE EVIL FACE OF CYBERSPACE

Cyberspace provides a new avenue and new media for criminals to cause harm. Increasingly, crimes in the physical world tend to be, well, more physical. In general, cyber criminals deploy sophisticated technology in what are, quite often, very elaborate schemes. Cyber crimes can include a physical side, but most do not.

Subtle cyber attacks elude detection, for months, and maybe even years. Criminals cloak themselves in veils of legitimacy, which makes wicked plots difficult to uncover and stop.

In cyberspace, criminals become social engineers and create scenarios that mimic real life. Cyber adversaries manipulate victims to unwittingly expose themselves to crimes and trick victims into actions they would never make if the true intent of those actions were known.

Through consumer education efforts, more users warily approach emails phishing for personal information (but as we saw from the Nigerian example, email scams still work).

Here's another crazy but true scenario. A bored cyber criminal trolls the Internet looking for information on the conference happening across town. A little sleuthing reveals the name of the keynote speaker's personal assistant. A simple program spoofs the hotel conference phone, and the adversary calls the assistant to inform him or her that the speaker's billing information is incorrect. The assistant is tricked into revealing financial information. Our cyber crook acts lightning fast, using the stolen card data far and wide, turning a tidy profit before the next bank statement arrives. Sound implausible? It happens.

I once worked a case for a manufacturer targeted by a foreign adversary. For more than three years, an adversary attempted to steal product details worth billions of dollars. The hackers focused on the CEO as the main avenue into the computer network, targeting his accounts for months. The adversary performed extensive reconnaissance, waiting for an opportunity to strike, and knew everything about the executive: where he grew up, details about his family, his address, and even where his kids went to school.

The adversary got its opportunity: there was an accident at the high school the CEO's son attended. The adversary did not cause the accident, but operatives monitored any news potentially relevant to the CEO. Within forty-five minutes of the accident, the CEO received an email:

> Dear concerned parent,
> As you know there was an accident this morning at Eagle Ridge High School. Our utmost and primary concern is the safety of all children involved. While we understand your concern, please refrain from coming to the high school because we are in lockdown as order is restored. Attached is emergency contact information with additional incident details.
> We appreciate your continued support,
> Sincerely,
> The Superintendent of the School District

With no spelling or grammatical errors, this email appeared to come from the school system. The attachment appeared on school letterhead and contained all the proper information for the school, the hospital, and the police department. It looked legitimate.

Six months later, the company detected unusual traffic on its network, and my security firm investigated. We tracked the suspicious activity to the CEO's computer, and specifically to the "superintendent's" email attachment. The false communication contained malicious code, opening a backdoor in the company's network for the foreign adversary to steal proprietary information.

Now be honest, if you are a parent, and you received that email, you would open the attachment. You are also thinking, I am not a CEO with a billion-dollar secret. But this executive's company invested $15 million in cybersecurity. How much do you invest in your online protection? The average user represents a simple target, and if you digitally store sensitive information, beware. Trust me.

Attackers launch less time-intensive campaigns against typical users, but those assaults are just as effective. While individual data might not be worth a lot by itself, combine the bank account numbers and personal information of 5,000,000 other users, and the value starts to build. Even if just one in 1,000 accounts yields monetary gain, the illicit profits add up.

How many times have you received a call from a credit card company investigating unusual activity on your account?

What is the first thing they ask? They want you to verify your identity and to provide personal information to do that. Chances are, the call is legitimate, but you should always be suspicious. Ask callers to verify *their* identity by providing you with details about the company. If they cannot do that, or you have any doubt, hang up and call the credit card company on your own. Use the fraud phone number located on the back of your card. Do NOT provide any data until you are convinced the call is for real.

You are a target, and the adversary is clever. Make sure you are careful and clever, too.

EVIL EVOLVES

Cybersecurity adapts almost as rapidly as evil; effective security is not static. Secure today, gone tomorrow. And even as fundamental principles of security do not change, cybersecurity solutions must evolve like opponents. Adversaries do not want to be caught, and defenders do not want to be caught with their pants down.

Adversaries and defenders study each other. When the good guys ferret out hacker techniques, those entry points slam shut. When a specific type of cyber attack no longer works, adversaries learn what defenses security specialists use and adjust their attacks to circumvent the defenses or find another entry point. We find ourselves on the African savannah again, with the lions and gazelles: everyone runs.

Let me reveal the scariest part about cyberspace natural selection. Unlike visible and annoying primeval cyber assault, today's attacks stealthily gain persistent access and zero in on valuable data.

SCRIPT KIDDIES

In the mid-to-late 1990s, as Internet use grew more mainstream, tech-savvy teenagers became fascinated with hacking. It developed into a sport or a hobby for many young adults.

Many of those early hacks were the work of younger kids showing off their skills or protesting some alleged injustice. While defacing a website causes degrees of embarrassment to an organization, early attacks caused little, direct harm or long-term financial impact. Those were the days!

At that time, ecommerce was in its infancy, and most websites only provided static information. More importantly, sites were NOT connected to back-end databases that contained large amounts of sensitive data. Early hacks were often dismissed because cyber forensics barely existed, and minors usually committed the crimes.

Plus, kids were kids. They did not possess technical expertise, and they shared or copied the same hacking scripts. The term "script kiddie" emerged, referring to kids who used pre-written scripts and blindly ran them against targeted sites. Networks at the time employed default operating systems, which meant many sites across the Internet were configured in the same manner. So even though the person running the script often did not know how it worked, the scripts just worked.

At the same time, the hacking elite arose. Elite hackers differentiated themselves from script kiddies as programmers who actually understood what they were doing; adversaries able to improvise and write new code to break into systems. However, the Internet was based on information sharing, so very often these scripts, even though they took tremendous work, were freely distributed as proof of concept.

Ultimately these predictable exploits acted upon predictable systems, and signature detection stood as the traditional defense. Every piece of code has a unique binary string that represents the code, similar to a fingerprint with a human. (Remember binary code, those 1s and 0s?) By identifying the unique fingerprint of a piece of malicious code, software could detect it on all systems. Today, this defense is less effective because adversaries continually alter how they break into systems. So while traditional, endpoint security software represents a good start, cyber behaviors need to change.

ADVANCED PERSISTENT THREATS

The definition of advanced persistent threat (APT) is often misunderstood. It refers to the new types of attacks that are targeting you and trying to steal information.

The "A" in APT does not stand for the advanced nature of the attack, but rather it stands for the advanced nature of the adversary. The adversary may use the quickest, easiest, and most effective methods to create chaos online. Today that method is sending a well-crafted email that looks legitimate and tricks the recipient into clicking on the attachment, which infects their system. This type of attack is known as a phishing attack. Therefore, it is important to remember that even though the adversary is advanced, the methods of compromise are often simple and straightforward.

The "P" refers to persistent, which means the adversary will continuously try to break into your system. You are always under attack. When you are connected to the Internet, you should always be on guard.

The "T" stands for the stealthy, targeted, and data focused threats of a skilled adversary. Hackers do not want to be visible, and they do not want to get caught. Instead of receiving an email from your boss that says, "I love you," which is obviously fake, now you will receive an email from your boss with the subject "Please review before the next status meeting," which looks very legitimate. Today's advanced threats are hard to detect.

TOOLS OF EVIL

The real people behind advanced threats do not look at their work as an attack, but rather as a mission, with clear objectives and goals.

With little fish like you and me, attacks are not personal. Your personal information is identified by a number, not your name. You are just one face in a crowd of 5, 10, 50, or 500,000,000 targets. If you employ strong cyber hygiene, you can lower your odds of being in that crowd. Will you be the lion? Or will you be the gazelle?

In mega-data breaches, hackers attack personal users with advanced threats: malicious code delivered via email, bogus web links known as drive-by downloads, or watering-hole attacks in which malware infects popular websites. Again, we have already covered many ways you can minimize your online risk—employ those methods.

VIRULENT VIRUSES

Viruses reign as the most common type of malicious code, a parasitic piece of software that attaches itself to an executable file. Executable files perform activities. Word processing programs and spreadsheet applications are examples of very common executables. In the case of a virus, a malicious activity infects a system or application.

The Barney Fife security perspective perceives virus protection as easy: do not introduce new executables into your system. For those of us that are not Level 5 dungeon masters, let me make it clear. DO NOT OPEN ANY ATTACHMENTS IN AN EMAIL. Security gets complicated when people make it harder than it needs to be. If you keep it simple, you become secure.

The rule is simple, but we degenerate to madcap Mayberry when we come across exceptions and bad habits. It requires training, but for rules to work, permit zero exceptions. Strict compartmentalization allows connectivity while reducing risk to critical data. For example, many corporations and government agencies maintain devices connected to the Internet but not connected to internal networks. Conversely, devices connected to internal networks do not connect to the Internet.

Bad habits often break rules. Some click-happy users check out every hyperlink they see. It is almost as if they cannot help themselves. You must retrain your brain to make safer cyber behavior your new habit. Your first step? Set up your mail client, or install software, to block all attachments.

Attachment addicts, before you throw your arms up in the air, secure alternatives to attachments do exist. You can still exchange data without opening attachments. Remember, cybersecurity offers options; find the one that best meets your functionality and safety objectives.

Email, an unauthenticated means of communication, was never meant to be a medium to exchange documents. Spoofing email addresses and adding rogue attachments must be the basics that are taught in Introduction to Hacking.

Conversely, most of us do need to exchange files. File-sharing services offer stronger security than simply emailing attachments. With file sharing, both users create accounts with the service (usually available on a website and an app) and then upload and access shared files. These applications employ robust cyber defense, and users determine with whom they will share files, resulting in a more reliable way to exchange files.

Death to the attachment!

I do not endorse any specific file-sharing services, but you'll find plenty of good ones online. Remember, I maintain that everything is "hackable." Once again, you must balance acceptable risk with desired outcomes.

SLIMY WORMS

The terms virus and worm are not synonymous; they act differently, albeit with similar goals. Viruses reside within executable files requiring activation (that fatal click when you view an attachment).

Worms are automatic; an adversary creates automated code with the sole purpose of breaking into systems. Worms typically target servers or systems directly visible on the Internet. But personal devices should not be directly visible, so most users and personal machines should be more concerned with viruses.

To be safe, if you have personal Internet access at your home, install a firewall appliance to protect all of your personal devices. Firewall appliances are often sold as a DSL/cable modem router and can cost as little as $50.

These appliances allow any of your devices to initiate outbound connections to the Internet, but do not allow anyone from the Internet to directly access your internal systems, a simple and easy trick to protect against worms. Warning: firewalls do not stop email traffic, so firewalls will not stop viruses hidden in those communications.

MODERN DAY TROJAN HORSES

A digital Trojan horse resembles the wooden Trojan horse the Greeks used to trick the people of Troy, although with less wood and more malicious code. A Trojan horse disguises its true purpose. An online adversary sends a target that looks to be a legitimate program. (Have you noticed I keep repeating this idea? It *looks* legitimate. It *looks* safe. Cyber warriors master the art of deception.)

Maybe the Trojan horse takes the form of a cool game or funny video. Bottom line, Trojan horses hide elaborate tricks. When you run the cool game or click play on the video, little do you know that in the background, a covert program launches and infects your system.

To avoid a Trojan horse, practice the same cyber hygiene recommended to avoid viruses: never open attachments. Instead, use file-sharing services and embrace a healthy dose of paranoia.

There are many different types of malicious code. This section was just meant to give you a flavor, and offer some techniques for users to protect their systems from being infected.

NEXT GENERATION MALWARE AND RANSOMWARE

While not born into the digital world, many adults today are fully, digitally immersed. Think back to the early days of computing, when malware constituted a system's biggest threat.

Early malware aimed to cause chaos, not necessarily to steal. Malicious codes like *Melissa, I Love You, Code Red,* and others disrupted businesses, and indirectly cost companies money via lost productivity. As annoying as those early bugs were, companies could recover with minimal losses.

Not so today. Cyber adversaries want money or access to other valuable assets. A million stolen credit card numbers bring a tidy sum on the black market. Adversaries rewrite the game plan and monetize cyber attacks. A consumer's primary cyber concern now is protecting passwords and locking down financial accounts, not preventing service slowdowns.

Ransomware is a particularly vicious strain of malware. In these attacks, adversaries hold digital information hostage and release it only for a ransom. This type of attack will only get more dangerous, as more adversaries seek new ways to monetize their criminal activities. Cryptolocker, a particularly malicious piece of code, attacked Windows systems in 2014. It tricked users to click on code disguised as safe content, rendering devices useless until a ransom was paid.

Many users sidestep ransom demands because they back up all critical data on their machines on a regular basis. Always operate under the premise that your system could be made unusable at any time, and employ a secondary level of backup. The second level can be anything from a portable hard drive purchased at any electronic store to cloud-based backups.

The bottom line: if you only own one copy of your data, consider yourself hosed.

CHRONIC CONDITIONS

What exactly do viruses, worms, and Trojan horses try to do? A lot of sneaky stuff.

Sometimes, infecting and shutting down systems is a vicious act perpetrated by fraudsters who want to prove they can defeat intricate cyber defenses and cause mayhem. Notoriety. That elusive fifteen minutes of fame.

Or, the end game is about acquiring personally identifiable information to exploit for financial gain.

Obsession. Compulsion. Abduction. Even vengeance. Scary, but more and more, these crimes contain a cyber angle.

As the world digitizes crucial data, we will see more and more crooks holding crucial data hostage, until financial demands are met.

THE BLACK MARKET OF EXPLOITS

At the next party you attend, throw out the term "dark web." It sounds really cool and makes it sound like you know a lot about cybersecurity. The dark web is a part of the Internet only accessible to those who know how to find it, hidden in dark, digital recesses, often only accessible with special software and specific cyber connections. It might be a fun place for super-cyber eggheads to play, but the dark web mostly serves as a hotbed of criminal activity.

It is the black market of exploits, where adversaries sell compromised information, exchange attack methods, share known vulnerabilities in networks or software, and collaborate to breach tough cyber defenses. When major retailers are breached, stolen credit cards are sold in large batches to the highest bidder. Sadly, a lot of child pornography is exchanged on the dark web. Organized gangs of hackers and other criminals communicate covertly, and now even terrorists exploit the dark web. Quite often, it is where the worst cyber attacks are launched, and it is quite a scary place.

READY, SET, GO!

Technology enables endless opportunities. Technology also makes parenting mind-numbingly scary. All hope is not lost. If you understand the dangers, risk can be contained.

Never mistake cyberspace as a beautiful and simple place, where unicorns drift through fields of daisies, while spreading fairy dust and rainbows in their wake.

The Internet is not a safe place to work, live, and do business—evil is lurking behind every email and website, waiting to turn you into a victim. Cyberspace is complex and filled with disease.

Inoculate yourself, your family, your organization, and your systems.

Here is what you need to remember to earn your cybersecurity black belt:

+ Cyberspace is often a cheap copy of real life, where criminals mimic real life to dupe victims. Verify, and then verify again, everything you come across in cyberspace.

+ Adversaries are the yin to the defenders' yang. When the bad guys discover a weakness, they exploit it. When the good guys find the weakness, they fix it. It is a vicious cycle.

+ Advanced Persistent Threat (APT) refers to the idea that cyber dangers are not always technically complex, but they are smart and relentless.

✦ Cyber viruses are actually short programs attached to files, designed to cause damage when activated. The safest way to avoid infection when sharing documents and other types of attachments is to use a file-sharing service.

✦ Worms are different from viruses; they do not require interaction with users. Instead, worms attempt to break into systems. At home, protect your systems from worms with a firewall appliance.

✦ Have we learned nothing from history? Trojan horses hide in the background of legitimate-looking files, infecting your system before you know what is happening. Like with viruses, file-sharing services can also protect devices from Trojan horses.

✦ Malware is any type of computer code meant to cause damage on a system. Ransomware attacks are on the rise; attackers hold digital information hostage until the victim pays for its release.

✦ Protect yourself from any cyber attack, and especially ransomware attacks, by backing up your critical data.

✦ The dark web is an Internet playground for criminals, where cyber attacks are planned and stolen information is sold to the highest bidder.

CHAPTER 5

YOU ARE THE TARGET

Twenty-four hour cable news channel headlines scream about alleged state-sponsored cyber attacks. Did Chinese hackers really try to steal trade secrets? Did Russian adversaries attempt to influence the elections?

While large corporations and government agencies rank high as popular cyber targets, you and your family should not breathe a sigh of relief. Cyber adversaries stalk you and your family, too, with financially-driven attacks or predatory overtures threatening personal safety.

SHOOTING YOURSELF IN THE FOOT

The actions of a typical cyberspace visitor constitute the greatest threat to personal cybersecurity. Skilled cyber adversaries, especially stalkers and child predators, scan the Internet trolling for targets. Something as innocent as posting a picture of your children on vacation can put your child in a predator's crosshairs.

By looking at your social media profiles, and those of your children, predators build fairly accurate pictures of intended victims, and use that information to build dangerous virtual relationships.

With knowledge as simple as knowing where a parent works, a cyber predator can claim to be a co-worker, and strike up an online friendship with an unsuspecting youngster. Children are very smart but also very innocent and trusting.

Clearly the social media cat is not going back into the bag. So I want you to ask yourself some tough questions every time you go online. Think about cyberspace differently and always consider the impact your social sharing can have on your family.

LOCK IT UP, TURN IT OFF

Admit it, you have been guilty of walking away from a computer or laptop, leaving it on and accessible to anybody who walks by. Never, ever do that again. At best, your teenager sends an email to your wife claiming he has an extended curfew. Worst case scenario, someone uses your login to commit a crime.

When you walk away from your computer or device, lock it. On Windows this is as simple as holding down the Windows key as you press the letter L.

But the danger does not end there. When your electronic device is on and connected, it is a potential target. First, an adversary can remotely access your computer. Second, any malicious software that may have been installed could be communicating on the Internet—sending sensitive information from your files to an adversary.

When you leave your device for an extended time—the end of a workday or when you go to bed—turn it off. Do not offer an adversary ten to twelve hours of uninterrupted time to hack your unmonitored computer. If your computer is turned off, not only is it not a target but it cannot communicate.

Effective cybersecurity reduces the attack vector. Turning off your computer is a simple but effective method and makes it more difficult for the adversary. Here are more essential steps to building a cyber defense:

Limit the details you give away online. Never post your address, current location, or the school you or your kids attend. This requires some mental retraining because many social media users want to let their networks know about the cool places they frequent. Social media connects people, and the instinct is often to share contact information. Stop it.

Anytime you share online, ask yourself: What is the positive benefit of sharing? What is the downside of sharing? Can this information be used to cause harm to my family or me? Most importantly, can I live with the potential consequences or losses?

Verify and validate associations. Hopefully at this point, I have convinced you that not everyone is who he or she says they are online. A forty-year-old creepy dude can pose as a sixteen-year-old teenager. A crazy ex can pose as a high school friend to monitor and track your activity.

"Trust but verify" is the key component of virtual relationships. My virtual friendship philosophy rests on the belief that if you went ten years without talking to someone, you can go another ten years without talking to them, and your life will be just fine. I am not antisocial. I just do not believe people need validation from the number of virtual followers or friends they can collect. Verify all questionable online identities through other friends or phone calls.

Err on the side of caution. Cyber users need to make conscious decisions about their online visibility. If you want everyone to know every detail of your life, and you are willing to accept exposure to cyber stalkers, then choose and live out that online persona. Or maybe not.

When my friends and colleagues are surprised by how much I know about them, I understand they did not consciously consider the pros and cons about online sharing. They have shared more than they realized. By the same token, I always laugh when Hollywood stars post every detail about their lives but then complain about a lack of privacy.

Talk to your family about risks. Parents, talk to your children, and children, talk to your parents. Both sides have unique knowledge to share. Parents carry experience, and let's face it, children often better understand how technology works.

Either way, any parent knows the key to successful parenting is communication. Be a successful parent online. A conversation about social sharing might be as painfully embarrassing as that talk about the birds and bees, but do not avoid it. When children understand the reasons behind their parents' concerns, there is a better chance that dangerous, online-behavior patterns can be broken.

IDENTITY THEFT GROWS UP

In the 1990s, consumers learned to shred important financial documents, put trash outside right before delivery, and never, ever just tear in half those preapproved credit offers.

However, identity theft evolved, and online crimes now thrive in cyberspace. On the dark web's black market, millions of stolen credit card numbers exchange hands like commodities on the stock exchange. Consumers keep multiple credit cards just so they have access to credit when, not if, one of their cards is compromised and turned off.

One day these massive financial data breaches will be the most dangerous threat to your online personal security. Large corporations bear the brunt of financial losses in those cases. But for now, small gangs and lone wolves, surfing the web looking for easy identities to pluck off, constitute your greatest cyber menace.

Cyber criminals empty bank accounts, illegally apply for credit cards, and destroy financial reputations with just a few keystrokes. According to federal research from the Bureau of Justice Statistics, more than two-thirds of identity theft victims report a direct financial loss.[1]

From the ubiquitous free WiFi to insecure home networks, and even strangers glancing over your shoulder while waiting for a latte—threats bombard your personal, digitized data. Even if you deploy the two-device defense discussed earlier in this book, all of your data needs to be protected the same way.

How can you put a padlock on your digital identity? Passwords—good, strong passwords.

PASSWORD COMPLEXITY AND PERPLEXITY

Just about everyone uses at least one password; some people have upwards of ten. Password diligence and best practices deteriorate as people view them as a necessary evil but also as a nuisance. It's very tempting to use just one or two easy-to-remember passwords, but weak passwords bear a large part of the blame for online security breaches.

Online security depends on generating strong passwords for different accounts. A password is your virtual key—protect it. Just as you would not leave your house key taped to your front door, do not leave your passwords on a sticky note hanging from your computer monitor.

A simple technique to create strong combinations: paraphrase, instead of copying. Pick a phrase that you will always remember, and use the first letter of every word in that sentence in your password.

For years, I used M1swb@GH@9:15 as one of my strongest passwords. How did I remember this string of numbers, letters, and characters?

M — My

1 — 1st

s — son

w — was

b — born

@ — at

G — Georgetown

H — Hospital

@

9:15

Paraphrasing generates passwords that are easy to remember but hard for the adversary to guess. Remember these guidelines:

✦ Use a combination of letters and numbers—never use only one or the other.

✦ Stay away from using names of spouses, children, or pets.

✦ Use a bizarre combination of words that only you would remember.

✦ Do not use your phone number or birthday—these are considered "weak" passwords.

VARIETY IS THE SPICE OF LIFE

Password1, Password123, and 1password are essentially the same password, in the eyes of a cyber crook. So many users use the same password across multiple accounts or make simple modifications to the same password for different accounts. And the adversary knows this, and will try variations of common passwords or your personally identifiable information to crack passcodes.

Mix up your passwords; you never want to make it easy to be compromised.

At the same time, we all know the frustration of being locked out of an online account after incorrectly entering a password. Is this the password with the number sign at the end? Or is it the case-sensitive version of your favorite baseball team?

Driven by the need for secure, easy-to-use passwords, cybersecurity software enables the basic user to create powerful personal protection.

Expect more online applications to roll out one-time passwords (OTPs), valid for only one login attempt. OTPs often include two-factor authentication requiring users to verify identity in two different ways. OTPs are generated and applied by a website or are communicated to users via email or text. Combining one-time passwords with user credentials makes it very difficult for an adversary to cause harm. In the rare case an OTP becomes compromised, it can only be used once, limiting damage.

Password vaulting programs also strengthen password security. Vaulting stores all of a user's passwords, requiring two-factor authentication for access. These applications allow users to generate complex passwords, or the program can also randomly create difficult passcodes. Instead of remembering several intricate PINs, consumers only need remember the combinations to the vault's two-factor authentication to access all stored passwords.

WHAT WAS THAT AGAIN?

Now that you have all of these strong and fancy new passwords, you will never forget any of them, right?

Just kidding, of course. Everybody forgets a password now and then. But whatever you do, be exceedingly careful with how you reset forgotten passwords. If you receive an unsolicited email about resetting your password or notifying you of suspicious activity on any account, never click on any links contained in that message.

Instead, you should always go directly to the trusted corporate or retail website, hopefully already bookmarked in your web browser, and check your account. Password scams are quite common, and if you give away your password to an account, you are handing a cyber adversary access to all of your personal information stored on that site.

FORGET ABOUT IT

So you know those little boxes that pop up when you visit your favorite websites, so kindly offering to "Remember Me" or to allow the site to access your location? Well, they really are not so helpful as you may think.

When you enable those functions, the "remembered" information, such as your user name or passwords, is stored on your device with a minimal level of security. Anyone who gains access to your device or system can potentially crack your passcodes and access your accounts with that information. Many people use the same or similar passwords across multiple sites, so when an adversary gets access to one password, it can be easy for them to figure out your other passwords.

Even riskier than allowing a website to store a password is saving a credit card number online. Many credit card scams today are focused on skimming, a so-called "low and slow" attack. Criminals want to evade detection, so they do not charge—and you will not see—a $40,000 unauthorized charge on your credit card account.

For most of us a $40,000 charge is an unusually high purchase, and fraud detection software and other security measures flag that type of transaction. Not to mention that a consumer using good, old-fashioned manual analysis—that is, someone reviewing individual charges—would definitely notice such a large charge when the monthly credit card statement came in the mail (or via email link).

But imagine an extra $5, $10, or $20 charge from vendors who may already be familiar to you. A smaller, fairly typical—but definitely unauthorized—charge like that might slip by you. It might not seem like a lot of money. But think of it this way. An adversary manages to charge $10 to 3,000 different, individual accounts. When you do the math—all those small, unauthorized charges add up to a not-so-little, illegal profit of $30,000. And, when cyber criminals get away with the same scams every month, they build a very nice, not-so-small income stream. And, truth be told, even that number—$30,000 a month—is a relatively small loss in the credit card business.

WHAT'S IN YOUR CYBER WALLET?

The convenience of free shipping, lower prices, and the ability to avoid the shopping mall are unbeatable advantages to shopping online. I will not even try to tell you not to do it. But I insist you maintain separate credit cards for online purchases.

If you limit cyber and recurring charges to a handful of credit cards, it will be easier to pinpoint the source of fraudulent charges. I used to have a card with fraudulent charges every month. I looked at the two or three places I used that card online and tracked down which vendor was the source of the unauthorized charges. When I changed credit cards and stopped doing business with that seller, the fake charges stopped.

Please set strict spending limits on the cards you use online. It would not be prudent to cyber shop with your ultra-platinum card that carries a sky-high credit limit. Consider what the card will be used for and contact the card provider to set appropriate spending limits. While most consumers are fortunately able to prove fraudulent charges, you do not want $10,000 in counterfeit purses sitting on your credit report until you can prove your innocence.

The more protection you can employ to guard your financial information, the better off you will be. Some financial institutions even offer virtual credit card features, which utilize two-factor authorization to keep your "real" credit card number separate from your virtual number. Virtual card number generators can usually be accessed via the web or as a program downloaded to your device. As you make purchases or donations, you can set up virtual numbers for single-use or multiple-use. You can further protect your accounts by setting strict spending limits on transactions made with the virtual credit card numbers.

Over the next several years, as cyber breaches continue to cause harm and organizations pay more attention to online security, you should be on the lookout for more security features that can help protect your online persona and accounts. But no matter the number or comprehensive qualities of additional security features, you cannot let your guard down. All the security in the world does not help if you do something stupid.

TO YOUR CREDIT

Corporations suffering massive data breaches typically offer victims free subscriptions to credit bureau reports. Many, many, many of you reading this book probably receive that access. Are you using it?

Did you know that every consumer is entitled to free, yearly credit reports, under the Fair Credit Reporting Act regulation?

Consider buying additional reports on a frequent basis. The sooner a financial anomaly is discovered, the sooner it can be resolved. Credit reports contain all credit accounts in a person's name, hopefully making it quite easy to identify suspicious activity.

Comb those reports for mistakes. My assistant shares the same first and last name with her sister-in-law, and every few years, she finds her relative's fifteen-year-old debt on her credit report.

BE A SCOUT

If you were ever a scout as a child, you know the motto, "Be Prepared." Note these two websites, so when you become the victim of a breach (remember, no ifs here), you are ready to start the process of recovery with some free resources:

✦ **AnnualCreditReport.com**. This is not some crazy television infomercial. By law, the nation's largest credit reporting services are required to provide all consumers with one free credit report per year. This site allows you to request reports from TransUnion, Experian, and Equifax. This is the official, government-sanctioned website. Do not be fooled by other services claiming to do the same thing.

✦ **IdentityTheft.gov.** The federal government maintains resources dedicated to helping victims of identity theft. The site contains checklists, sample letters, and concrete steps for victims to recover from a cyber breach.

CHECKING-IN EQUALS CHECKING UP

Reservations at the hottest restaurant in town! The Little League championship and Junior is on the mound! Exciting moments to be shared online!

When users identify their locations on social media, they voluntarily reveal to friends—and potential cyber foes—where they are. And sometimes, even more importantly, they reveal where they are not. This type of personal information also helps adversaries track your daily routines, and amounts to valuable intelligence about your life. Why would you give that away?

Cyber shoppers unwittingly reveal their locations to marketers when they enter a zip code to find the closest gas station, or track down the store that has the hot new pair of sneakers in size eleven.

Be aware and be careful when using location services. I think we can all agree that broadcasting your daily schedule is unwise. We will talk more about cyber spying in a later chapter.

ARE YOU AN ADDICT?

Turn off your phone, put it in a drawer, and do not use it for forty-eight hours.

How did you do? How long did you make it without your phone, without texting or email before you started getting anxious or freaking out? Maybe you did not even try because you thought this exercise

was useless, or it just was not practical or possible for you to do.

You may be an addict. Addicted to technology.

Adversaries know this and are now targeting electronic devices and electronic communication. From a financial-fraud, identitytheft, or sensitive-information perspective, your phone—with its contents—is probably one of the most valuable assets that you own.

What do mobile users store on their devices? Credit cards numbers, driver's license information, bank accounts, passwords, and other very critical information. Hapless celebrities, and jilted significant others, know the horror of their very personal pictures being splashed across the Internet.

Your phone places all of this personally identifiable information at risk. Evaluate if excessive online time is worth the potential exposure.

AIRPLANE MODE

Perhaps you travel frequently and turn your phone to airplane mode as the jet taxis down the runway. Have you ever thought about putting your phone in airplane mode when it is not critical for people to know exactly where you are? Especially when you have access to a landline telephone, or you are turning in for the night? Airplane mode offers another, convenient level of protection.

DOUBLE YOUR DATA

If you have a phone or tablet with no personal information on it and that device is lost, beyond laying out the cash for a pricey new device, you incur minimal losses. But if your device contains a large amount of critical data, you better go buy aspirin for your new and very large headache. Not only do you have to worry about potential harm, how will you get back all of your records?

Back up your data, frequently, on a device that rarely connects to the Internet. A backup minimizes the damage of missing data, but again, only if you back up your devices on a regular basis.

From a functionality perspective, you want data in many places. From a security and personal protection standpoint, you want data in a minimal number of places. Achieve balance with these conflicting strategies by focusing on the access and storage of the information.

SPLIT THE EXPOSURE

When separate pieces of your data are stored in multiple locations, you limit the consequences from an individual attack. If the email account you use for banking is breached, the tax records you store in the cloud are still protected.

I cannot conceive of a way the entire Internet could be compromised at the same time, so when you split your data, you split your potential for losses.

Also split your personality. I operate several email addresses, using different email clients. I have email accounts for my consulting business, the students I teach, and even a separate address for my friends and family. If one account goes down, only one part of my life is affected.

LOCAL VERSUS REMOTE

Cyber users choose from one of two backup options: local or remote.

Users keep local backups, like a removable hard drive or other physical form of storage, on hand—in their office, at the house, in a briefcase.

Users control the backup device, prohibiting any remote access. But do not stop there. I go crazy when I see a backup drive sitting casually on a bookshelf or acting as a paperweight on a cluttered desk. Invest in a small safe, preferably a portable, fireproof safe.

You are thinking that I am being paranoid again. But physically safeguarding your digital data is a worthwhile investment. Plan for the unexpected. The burglary, the house fire, or your kids' nosy friends: lock up the backup hard drive.

Far more prevalent than local backups, the lion's share of backup data resides in the cloud, a remote backup. "Cloud" is really just a fancy term to refer to systems that are accessible from the Internet.

Cloud-based solutions include applications like online banking, ecommerce, and social media sites. The public and private sector turn to cloud-based solutions because they are easy to implement, use, and maintain. A third-party provides storage and security. The only task left to users is to manage access, in the form of passwords.

A BOAT WITH A VIEW

Increased security demands we change our vantage point. Just because you do not see the adversary does not mean it does not exist; it just means you are not looking in the right place.

Many years ago I took my family with me to a speaking engagement in Hawaii. Along with a friend, we stole away for a few hours to enjoy a whale watching tour.

Sitting on the left side of the boat, I dreamily stared at the beautiful islands, wondering aloud if we might spot a whale. My friend twisted my head in the opposite direction, to the right side of the boat, where a majestic whale silently cut through the water. Without a new vantage point, I risked missing the whale.

Cybersecurity experts need to think like whale watchers. Approach problems from every perspective, not just the one directly in front. Once I changed my vantage point, I was able to see the whales.

Traditional security methods gaze at the wrong spot because they fail to think like an adversary. Be aware that cyber criminals disguise threats as legitimate-looking emails, websites, browser searches, hyperlinks, and social media posts. Do not click first, and ask questions later. Once an infection worms its way into your system, and your identity, it is too late to play it safe. Always measure twice, and click once.

READY, SET, GO!

Now you know, if you communicate electronically, you are the ideal cyber target. By taking a step outside of yourself, donning the lenses of a criminal, I guarantee you will finally be motivated to clean up your cyber hygiene. Realize you are the target, deploy basic cybersecurity protocols such as limiting exposure, establishing complex passwords, and creating data backups.

Change is hard; change is not your enemy. You can remove your identity from a direct line of cyber fire. Make time today to protect yourself and your family.

Here is what you need to remember to earn your cybersecurity black belt:

✦ Every time you enter cyberspace, you become the potential victim of a cyber attack.

✦ Carefully limit what you share online. Even the most innocuous details can be used against you.

✦ Always turn your electronic devices off when you are done using them. If you are only temporarily stepping away from your phone or computer, lock the screen. Never leave a device unsecured.

✦ Trust but verify. Take the time to verify the people you communicate with online are who they say they are.

✦ Start talking to your children early about safe online practices. Better late than never is unacceptable.

✦ Thanks to the Internet, identity theft is growing increasingly sophisticated.

✦ Maintain strong and separate passwords for all of your online accounts. Password paraphrasing will help you craft tough passwords that are easy to remember.

✦ Using similar passwords is as bad as using the same password for every account.

✦ Never click on password reset or suspicious activity links, unless you requested that material. Instead, visit a website directly when you receive those email requests.

✦ Ignore website and application features that offer to store your username, location, password, credit card information or any other personally identifiable information. Security for those "remember me" functions is often lacking.

✦ Use separate credit cards dedicated to online shopping and recurring charges. Implement spending limits, and carefully monitor bank statements. You are much more likely to suffer multiple $20 losses than a $20,000 loss.

✦ Check your credit reports on an annual basis. Major credit bureaus are legally required to provide consumers with one free report a year. Keeping an eye on your credit can help you detect fraud faster.

✦ Speaking of checking: never check-in online! Posting while at a restaurant or soccer game lets cyber adversaries know you are not home, and provides details about your daily routine.

✦ Technology is addicting. Take back control from your mobile phone and evaluate your digital habits. Is the time you spend in cyberspace worth it?

✦ Use the airplane mode on your devices when you do not need to be contacted or connected, but still feel the urge to play a game of solitaire.

✦ Back up your data—frequently—to minimize frustration and losses if your devices fail for any reason.

✦ Back up critical data in pieces, and store each piece in a different place. If one backup is compromised, only part of your data is impacted.

✦ Your two backup options are local and remote, also known as cloud-based. In later chapters we will explore which option is best for you.

---

[1] "Victims of Identity Theft, 2014." Bureau of Justice Statistics (BJS). September 27, 2015. Accessed January 4, 2017. http://www.bjs.gov/index.cfm?ty=pbdetail&iid=5408.

CHAPTER 6

SMILE, YOU'RE BEING RECORDED! PERMANENTLY.

There are no secrets—just varying degrees of privacy.

TRACKING PROGRESS

Ask almost anyone if they would be OK wearing a personal tracking device, and the immediate response is NO. Why, most people reply in horror, would anyone allow their activities and locations to be tracked?

However, that ship sailed from port years ago, and almost everyone in the digital world is being tracked. What is this ubiquitous device, so efficiently recording your every move? The mobile phone.

The military targets adversaries tracking individual mobile phones. Police track cell phones to solve routine crimes. Sadly, various criminal elements use the same technology.

Tech-savvy parents also use cell phones to keep tabs on their children.

In fact, unbeknownst to consumers, many digital devices track user locations. Oftentimes users are not given the option to disable tracking. Many popular applications, like mapping programs and ridesharing services, rely on location tracking. We leave a digital footprint, and the sooner we accept it, we can move to protect ourselves.

When was the last time you checked your cell phone to see what applications are installed and which ones are utilizing location tracking?

As I was writing this book, I checked my phone and was surprised to find sixteen apps, most of them preinstalled as a part of the operating system, track location by default.

Many location services provide users with value; not all tracking devices are harmful. But users need to be aware their locations are monitored, and remember that whenever there is functionality, there will be some risks.

The trick with all technology is to understand the pros and cons, and to create scenarios maximizing the pros while minimizing the cons. We live in a world where no one can make a mistake, because if you do, it will be recorded, monitored, and tracked.

WHO OWNS YOUR DATA?

This might sound like a simple question with an obvious answer. Not so fast. Everyone thinks they own their data, but in many cases, that is not necessarily true.

If you are not running your own mail or web server, probably true for most people, you do not own your data. Whoever ultimately owns the server, also owns the information located on it.

For example, if the third party hosting your pictures went out of business tomorrow, shutting down the servers with no notice, you would lose access to your stored photos. (As discussed earlier, keeping a local backup of all critical or important information is key to making sure you do not lose important information).

I know people love Google because of its email, storage, and all other kinds of cool widgets. But, ask yourself, why does Google offer all of that value for free?

Not out of the kindness of its corporate heart; Google turns a tidy profit. Google, and other successful digital ventures, recognized a long time ago that content is king. The company in possession of valuable content wins.

User acceptance agreements, often several pages full of legal and technical mumbo jumbo, outline what users, and companies, can and cannot do with information stored in software and applications.

Have you ever read an ENTIRE user acceptance agreement for any of the software and services you use? Consumers are accustomed to scrolling to the bottom of the agreement and clicking "I agree" before accessing updates and applications. Basically, users agree to all of the terms and conditions of a service, without having any clue about what those terms really mean.

If you have trouble sleeping, you should spend some time reading some user agreements. All kidding aside, periodically, take a look at what you are agreeing to. In many cases, users agree to allow stored information to be used for marketing and "other purposes."

To build trust, maintain loyalty, and comply with the few, existing legal regulations, it does behoove technology applications to defend user privacy and rights—to an extent.

So I will go out on a limb and assert that Google is not going to splash your email and personal photos across the Internet as part of some marketing scheme. But your stored information can and will be used for marketing purposes. Did you ever notice you receive advertisements aligned with your interests and geographical location?

Every third-party digital service is doing it, not just Google. And do not forget, users agree to it. Just know that when you use online applications and software, the data you reveal becomes controlled and owned by that third party. All of those services leave a digital footprint traceable back to you.

EMAIL—PUBLIC OR PRIVATE?

In technology, as in most things in life, there is the way things are supposed to work, and the way things actually work. What is theory, versus reality, when it comes to your email?

In theory, your email is private, accessed only by you. In reality, many other people can access your email.

Look at how email works. The average email user does not maintain a personal server. So, to send or receive email, a mail client, known to you as your email program, communicates with a mail server, that is, software installed on a server. The server's owner can access anything on a server, including all emails. Of course administrators are not supposed to peruse customer emails, but it only takes one rogue employee for your email to land in the hands of an adversary.

When an adversary compromises an email server, the bad guys gain access to all material on that server. Just look at recent breaches involving Hollywood executives, or even the last presidential campaign, and you see how compromised emails can cause significant reputational damage.

Face it—we have all written something silly in an email because we assumed our communications would remain confidential. For fun, go back a year and randomly look at some of the emails you sent. At the time, the notes made sense or seemed reasonable, but out of context, a year later, you probably want to smack your forehead. To be safe, treat your email as a public record, not a private form of communication.

EMAIL IS A LEGAL RECORD

Never forget email constitutes a legal record and can be admissible in legal actions, causing you problems not only in the courtroom, but the court of public opinion.

People sue people for the stupidest things. Family members get into disagreements, and sadly, couples get divorced. Consumers sue merchants, and vendors pursue delinquent clients. When gathering potentially damaging evidence, lawyers often go after email.

Pretend that your mother, religious leader, boss, or significant other is copied on every email you write. Better yet, imagine all of your so-called private communications will also be posted on social media. Do not get caught with emails down around your ankles.

A TRAIL OF BREADCRUMBS

Every time you use a connected device, you leave behind digital fingerprints and footprints. And, as we increasingly use technology for even the most mundane tasks in our lives, we leave behind a lot of clutter. Cyber adversaries are quick to sift through those breadcrumbs looking for potential exploits.

Think of a footprint; it is something you see. Mud tracked across a newly mopped floor. Fingerprints, on the other hand, are invisible; the marks your hands leave when you pick up that mop.

A digital footprint is deliberate; the data points users know they are leaving online—like when you post on social media, upload a resume to a recruitment site, or make a purchase online. Digital fingerprints can be harder to find, and users are often unaware they are leaving them behind.

As an expert witness, let me remind you, there are no secrets online. The unique way you operate in a digital world can be tracked and monitored.

The way you type on a keyboard and the methods you use to search for material on the web form unique behavioral patterns that cyber sleuths, both good and bad, use to follow users online. What you see on your favorite fictional television dramas actually happens in real life.

We have established it is next to impossible to delete your deliberate trail on the Internet; your fingerprint is even harder to erase. As a digital forensics witness, I have used digital fingerprints to find:

✦ A suspect's exact location (the crime scene) at the time of a murder.

✦ Pictures a user took and deleted over a year before.

✦ Wireless access points, proving a defendant illegally accessed a victim's WiFi.

- The location of two mobile phones over time, demonstrating a suspect stalked another individual.
- Two-year-old emails opened on a shared computer.
- Passwords, credit cards, bank accounts, and other personal information users believed were securely stored on their devices.

The last item should scare you because, unfortunately, cyber criminals often have access to methods and technology that I do not have. If I can do it, so can the bad guys.

YOU ARE WHAT YOU EAT

Parents often ask me why they see "unusual" or "inappropriate" ads as they surf the web. The answer is simple: you are what you eat. Think of ads on your computer as a virtual mirror, showing who you are and what you do in cyberspace. If you did not recently research shape wear, but the ads appearing on the family computer tout the benefits of leather over Lycra®, it might be time to talk to Junior.

The great marketers in the sky monitor and track your web surfing, and use that information to create your virtual identity. Your IP address and cookies, which are small pieces of code left in your system when you browse the Internet, let websites know who you are. So when you visit websites, background programs use your virtual identity to find ads that most closely match your persona.

If you use someone's computer and see inappropriate ads, that serves as a pretty good indicator of their online activity.

WHAT HAPPENS WHEN YOU HIT SEND?

Emails typically are stored in so many places, no matter how times you hit delete, a copy still exists somewhere. Before you hit send, ask yourself, do I want this message to live forever?

Many people falsely believe a deleted email ceases to exist. Anyone receiving your email has a copy. And we all know about the hazards of forwarding, and emails that wind up in the wrong mailbox.

Recalling an email does not mean anything. Very rarely does it work; recalls can be blocked. Short of breaking into a recipient's house and accessing their computer, options for truly deleting emails from other inboxes are limited.

Even if a recall worked, remember that your email is stored on a mail server, and these servers are backed up on a regular basis. Delete your emails locally, but most likely the server still has a retrievable copy.

Recognize that once you hit send, email lives forever. Email is emotionless, leaving readers free to interpret meaning. And not always the correct meaning.

Email might be a fast and easy way to communicate, but do not send any messages without some forethought. Focus on your content now, so it does not haunt you later.

WHAT HAPPENS WHEN YOU HIT POST?

I train all of my employees, family, and friends to pause before they post. Take a moment to consider potential repercussions of posting information. Once you hit post, very much like hitting send, your information becomes almost impossible to completely erase. By the time you delete a social media post, chances are it has already been viewed and saved in several locations.

I know many cases where people posted information and deleted those posts in as little as thirty minutes. But that information can still be found online today.

Yes, delete buttons exist, but once you send that content into cyberspace, you lose control of that information.

Never hop on social media when you feel emotional, sick, or somehow not in your typical frame of mind. When the human body gets upset, rational thought flies out the window, and people often do or say things they regret later.

Inappropriate social media posts cause fights, destroy friendships, and cost employees their jobs. In the digital world, emotions become permanent.

When I want to whip off a snarky note or share something crazy with a friend, I often write the message in a Word document, and review it the next day. Ninety-nine percent of the time, I enjoy a good laugh and delete the proposed message. Press pause on your social media habits; you will not regret it.

WHAT HAPPENS WHEN YOU HIT SAVE?

Take a step back to some basic computer technology. Your computer contains three key components: CPU, memory, and hard drive.

The CPU, or central processing unit, performs the calculations and processing necessary for your computer to function. The faster the CPU, the faster your system performs various functions.

A CPU uses memory to store the information actively used by your computer. When you are creating a word processing document, the information that appears on the screen is initially stored in memory. Memory is temporary, or what some people call "volatile." When you turn off your computer, anything in memory disappears.

Have you ever worked on a document and some sort of glitch erased all of your information before you hit save? You experienced first-hand volatile memory.

Finally, the hard drive, or hard disk, records your data when you click save. It is non-volatile or what some people call permanent storage. If you turn your computer off, any information on your hard drive will still be there when you turn your system back on.

So when you hit save, data is stored to your local hard drive, where information can be recorded and retrieved. Your hard drive is your gold mine, the safe that cyber criminals want to crack.

THERE IS NO DELETE BUTTON

The delete buttons on your devices and applications—they do not work. No, nothing is broken. But maybe we should rename the key "mostly deleted." Or the "deleted unless a cyber expert tries to find it" button.

Given the odds that almost everyone knows the gut-wrenching pain of digital loss, some examples even discussed in this book, you might find this news a bit confusing. But I have also demonstrated that restoration of seemingly lost files is possible.

I think I have also established that despite all of our best efforts, people will still do crazy things online. Hackers will break into systems. And now we face one other inevitability—digital permanence.

Pictures and videos on cell phones are like getting a tattoo in Vegas: it might seem like a really good idea at the time, but chances are, you are going to regret something. Some post, some comment, some picture—you will regret.

We are circling back to many themes examined earlier in this book, but I want to drive this point home: the Internet does not forgive, does not forget, and it punishes those that do not remember this.

THE REALITIES OF DELETION

Most computer users believe when they delete a document from their hard drive, it ceases to exist. And it might be true, for the average user. In reality, the pointer, or road map, to the document is deleted, but the data still resides on the computer. Someone who really knows how computers work can recover deleted information. Many programs and applications even now add extra layers of protection with automatic recovery features.

In Windows, when you delete a document, you will notice the amount of free space on your hard drive remains the same. Windows simply moves the deleted document to a new storage area, your recycle bin or trash, providing you with a safety net to recover files. Empty the recycle bin to make it harder, but not truly delete, a document.

Now there is no easy way for you to recover the information, but it still has not been deleted; the data remains on your hard drive and can potentially be recovered.

If you accidentally delete something and basic auto recovery features do not work, seek expert help. Do not try to recover it yourself by downloading and installing programs. Let me explain.

When you delete a document or empty the recycle bin in Windows, the data stays on your hard drive, but it is marked as free space. As long as you do not save anything new to the hard drive, all of your old data is still there.

However, when you start installing programs or saving information, your systems uses any free space that is available, meaning the deleted data can potentially be overwritten, making it even harder to recover. Notice I still hold out the possibility of recovery? Even at this stage, retrieval is possible.

I love to teach, and I travel to many conferences to train cybersecurity specialists. On a trip to New Orleans, I ran into a conference planner in tears. Trying to clear some space on her smartphone, she accidentally deleted all of her pictures: family weddings, grandchildren, holidays, and many other sentimental pictures disappeared.

I ascertained she did not try to recover the photos or download anything new since the deletion. Fortunately, I just came from a forensic gig and had all of my gear with me. I told her to stop crying and within five minutes, recovered all of her pictures.

The pictures were not actually deleted; they were just not accessible to her.

SECURELY DELETING INFORMATION

There are some ways to securely delete information, but they are usually beyond the reach of the typical digital user. Doctors, financial advisors, and other professionals often need to truly delete personally identifiable information. For this to work, you need to own all of the computers and servers that ever contained the data needing deletion.

Most of us own our laptops and devices, but do not own servers, and certainly not all of the servers our devices ever connect to on the Internet. If you have sensitive information that you want to control and permanently delete, only keep that data on local drives.

Once you know the information is only stored on your hard drive, programs exist to completely erase information. Secure delete programs overwrite files, so the data no longer exists. Be careful using these programs; if you make a mistake, you will not be able to recover information.

If you want to really get down into the weeds, yes, highly advanced adversaries might still recover the deleted information. Destroying a hard drive is truly the only foolproof method. Fortunately most of us are not in the crosshairs of those sophisticated cyber criminals.

A word of warning: secure delete programs can be downloaded from the Internet. We have already covered those dangers. Just because a program shows up in a browser search does not mean it can be trusted. Make sure that you have endpoint security software that scans all downloads, only go to trusted sites, and be super careful of what you install on your computer.

CLOUDY FORECAST

Online storage adds an interesting twist to saving and deleting information. When you log into many operating systems and applications, you actually log into a cloud-based service that automatically backs up your files. Every time you save a file, not only does a copy go to your hard drive (so you have the same problems outlined above), but a copy also goes to a third-party server backed up on a regular basis.

Even if you delete information from your hard drive, a copy, or even copies, remain on remote servers. When all copies are deleted from servers, information can still live on in backup files maintained by the vendor. In cyber forensics, I have worked on many legal cases, from domestic disputes to commercial cases, and successfully recovered files people believed to be long gone.

Online storage is invaluable for backing up information you never want to lose. Cloud services give you access to a level of backups and security you cannot achieve on your own. But it should only be used with data with minimal impact to you and your family if it were compromised. Use the cloud to back up family photos, articles, or schoolwork. Tax returns, bank statements, medical records, and other sensitive information might be better backed up on a portable drive you own and control.

CONTROL YOUR DATA, CONTROL YOUR DESTINY

On one hand, I am advising you to limit access and copies of your data to control data permanence. But I am also recommending how you can safely back up and maintain critical data.

One size does not fit all, even in cybersecurity. To truly be protected online, you need to have a well-thought-out strategy addressing the different needs of your different types of data. You need options. The general rule: the more sensitive the information, the more you want to control all access to it.

BACKUP OR NO BACKUP, THAT IS THE QUESTION

How do you strike a balance between backing up sensitive information and controlling copies of your data? After all, every backup is another data point requiring its own security.

If your critical data resides in only one location, you can more easily protect, control, and manage that information. Essentially the fewer locations you store your information, the easier it is to protect. On the flip side, if something happens to that data, you might not be able to recover or recreate it.

Think of a passport or driver's license. If you copy that information, you have more material to protect. But if a pickpocket swipes your wallet, getting identification replaced is easier when you have a copy of the original.

With your personal cybersecurity, I definitely recommend maintaining multiple copies of digital information. But not so many copies that you create unnecessary risk. Critical to keeping backups secure is ensuring the same level of security for every backup.

WHAT THE @$#%&^ IS ENCRYPTION?

Nothing makes you feel more like a cyber ninja than throwing around fancy words like encryption and cryptography. Although the words are often used interchangeably, they do mean slightly different things.

Cryptography is the science of creating coded, secure communications. Encryption is the actual complex mathematic algorithms or ciphers used to transform information with meaning into meaningless information. The good news is you do not have to understand any of that in order to utilize and gain the value of using cryptography, or crypto, as those in the know call it.

All you need to know is that crypto via encryption will take your digital information and make it so only authorized parties can read it. Encryption adds a strong layer of defense to your cybersecurity strategy.

If you do decide to store sensitive data on an Internet or cloud-based server, encrypt the information locally on your computer, and then upload only encrypted information. If someone gains access to private data, or steals your online credentials, they only have access to the encrypted information. Your files cannot be read or accessed without the encryption key, which explains the code used in the encryption process.

The security software that you install will include and take care of all the intricacies of encryption, so do not feel intimidated by these advance techniques. With user-friendly endpoint security software, users need only decide which information should be encrypted. Focus on the usability of encryption, not the mathematics, and you will be a pro in no time.

While not quite cryptography, I am fascinated by another form of covert communication: steganography. Steganography hides a message in plain sight. That is, inside seemingly innocuous pictures or media files.

Check out my book <u>Hiding in Plain Sight: Steganography and the Art of Covert Communication</u> and learn how the practice is a popular tool for secretly sending and receiving messages.

CHECK YOURSELF

Frequently review your social media and software security settings. In many cases, built-in defenses need to be turned on. Users find themselves caught off guard because they assume those features are turned on by default. Take the time to properly configure all security options available for your software and devices.

Your information security is your responsibility—not a vendor's responsibility. Yes, if a vendor deploys weak security defenses, they carry blame for a breach. But if you choose to use digital platforms, you must shoulder the risk that your information is no longer 100 percent secure.

DID YOU GET MY GOOD SIDE?

When your system is compromised, you lose more than personal data. You lose control over whatever applications and accessories are installed on your device, including the microphone and camera. If you do not need or regularly use either of those conveniences, which often are automatically included in new electronics, try to buy devices without any type of recording features. An adversary cannot attack something that does not exist.

But if you purchase systems with those features preinstalled, you should take the time to block or disable them. Not only can an adversary potentially access your camera or microphone, but also many programs will turn on those components without the user's knowledge. Truly, you can be recorded—audio or video recording— and you will not know it is happening. I cannot tell you how many times I am doing conference bridges via the web, and I have to remind people that their web camera is on because they were completely unaware it had been accessed.

If you need a camera or microphone on your devices, disable those features when you are not using them. Be sure to investigate security settings and limit the applications that can access audio-visual accessories. I see a lot of people cover their laptop cameras with a piece of tape or sticker, which is a step in the right direction.

But remember, the only foolproof way to protect yourself against being recorded is to go camera-less or microphone-less.

SPY ON YOURSELF

Spy on yourself and see what information you can find. Use a different computer, not the one you use every day, which already knows a lot about you. You can try some self-snooping from your own system, but compare the results from a system you have never used before.

Visit your favorite search engine and simply type in your name. Most people will be shocked by how much they can find.

If your first or last names are commonly used, add search qualifiers such as the state or city in which you live.

Most of my clients tell me they are casual Internet users and not a lot of information exists about them online. Celebrity or not, if you live in a digital world, you leave a digital footprint.

If you search and do not find any information, you did not look hard enough. Trust me on this. With the right tools, you will find information about yourself.

It is one thing for me to tell you about your digital footprint, but it is more valuable for you to see this first hand. Awareness is key to surviving online.

DVR FOR YOUR LIFE

When digital video recorder, or DVR, technology first came out, I thought it was the coolest thing in the world. Finally, I could watch TV shows when I wanted to, or pause a live broadcast while I put my kids to bed.

Good or bad, the Internet was designed with built-in DVR technology, and it cannot be turned off. Every online move you make lives somewhere, just waiting to be sent into syndication or played in endless reruns.

Be more selective about what you allow to be recorded. Be a cyber victor, not a cyber victim.

READY, SET, GO!

People live their cyber life the way they do their real life, which is very dangerous.

In the real world we can get mad and say things we do not mean, vent to a friend at dinner, and no one else will ever know what you said. In the real world you can live life out loud because despite the rise of recording and surveillance devices, there is no easy way for someone to find out everything that you say and do. But in cyberspace, you cannot hide.

Do not let your digital footprint wander into a swamp.

Here is what you need to remember to earn your cybersecurity black belt:

✦ Your mobile phone is a de facto tracking device. Check your security settings to limit which applications can use location-tracking services.

✦ Consumers typically do not own data they store on third-party servers. That means your emails, pictures, audio, video, and social media posts that you keep online do not technically belong to you.

✦ Back up locally anything you store online.

✦ User agreements might be filled with mumbo-jumbo, but if you blindly click "agree" without reading the terms of use, you are signing your life away.

✦ Your email account is NOT private. It can be accessed by your email provider, or compromised when hackers attack an email server.

✦ Email is a legal record and can be used in court. Use the same caution with electronic communication that you use with the written word.

✦ A digital footprint is the data users know they are leaving online, like a social media post, purchasing information, or electronic forms.

✦ A digital fingerprint is the data users do not know they are leaving online. It might be hard to find, but cyber experts can track digital fingerprints such as user location, when and where emails are opened, deleted photos, and more.

✦ Advertisers use your browsing history to determine which ads to display on the websites you visit.

✦ Consider email a permanent record. Even if you delete an email on your end, the act of transmitting and receiving creates copies of that communication. You also cannot control what a recipient will do with your emails. The same holds true with social media posts.

✦ When you press the save button on your computer, your data is stored on a hard drive.

✦ There is NO delete button. Cyber experts can often retrieve material deleted from hard drives and other storage devices. Most methods for successfully deleting digital material are beyond the reach of a typical cyberspace visitor.

✦ Online storage complicates the deletion conundrum. Cloud service providers routinely back up consumer data in multiple places.

✦ Find your happy place with backups. Balance your need to have copies of your data with the risk that comes with having multiple versions.

✦ Encrypt personal information stored on laptops and other mobile electronics. If a mobile device is lost or stolen, encrypted information makes it harder for an adversary to access stored data.

✦ Disable unnecessary microphones and camera. Yes, placing a small sticker or piece of tape over a laptop camera is actually a good idea. If you must use audio or video services on a device, make sure you turn off the camera or mic when not in use.

✦ Stop. Think. Type. Pause, asking yourself, "Is everything I typed absolutely necessary and how can this information be misconstrued?"

✦ Write and Wait. Type social media posts or craft emails, then walk away from the keyboard. A short break can provide clarity and save you from making comments that can come back to haunt you.

✦ Spying on your digital self is a great idea. Do it frequently and see what you can find about yourself online.

✦ Check your settings. Security functions and policies change frequently; stay on top of updates.

✦ Weigh your risks. What do you really want to entrust to the digital world? Balance the value of your information against the value you receive from online applications.

CHAPTER 7

CHILDPROOFING CYBERSPACE (FOR KIDS AND ADULTS!)

"Teach the children so it will not be necessary to teach the adults."

—*Abraham Lincoln*

Those of us of a certain age are quite grateful smartphones did not exist when we were college age—no need to have those exploits documented forever in cyberspace (whew!). But I worry about kids, and you should, too. You should have this conversation often with children (and yourself): what do I really want to reveal in cyberspace?

Kids need to be aware of the dangers and issues of living in cyberspace. Just as we teach our children not to talk to strangers, we need to engage with kids in frequent and open discussions about behavior in cyberspace.

Even with all the outlet plugs, bumpers, and safety latches available, kids still get hurt in the physical world. Cyberspace is no different, and in fact, can be near impossible to childproof. But let's never stop trying.

UNDERSTAND HOW IT WORKS

In order to have a meaningful discussion, we must start by understanding how kids use cyberspace. Digital technology now plays a large part in how children and teens communicate, whether via social media applications, email, texting, gaming, or web browsing.

You can certainly ask kids which applications they use, but I recommend looking at individual devices and researching installed applications.

Part of understanding how kids use cyberspace includes parents accessing the same platforms as their kids do, in order to monitor behaviors and to stay abreast of digital trends. If your child is on Facebook and Instagram, then you should be on those same media and connected to your child. You should be able to see all of their posts and interactions on every social media or messaging platform.

This might be more parenting advice than technical advice—follow your children online, but do not interact with them, at least in front of their friends. The mom who comments on her child's Instagram photo is today's equivalent of the pre-digital-age mom who chaperoned the homecoming dance in a frumpy dress, three sizes too small, and tried to twerk to gangsta rap. How embarrassing!

Yes, parent-to-child interactions on social media are that embarrassing to kids. And, you do not need to be a parenting expert (or cybersecurity expert) to know humiliation will not lead to open and honest discussion about cyberspace behaviors.

Do let your children know they are being watched, and quickly address any concerning behavior. But keep your public comments to a minimum.

TIME FOR A FAMILY MEETING

Talk to children frequently about cyber safety. What should you cover?

- ✦ Consider everything you do online to be public. If you would not say it in front of your grandmother, do not post it online. There are no secrets in cyberspace.
- ✦ There is no delete button in cyberspace. Even with applications that claim to quickly delete photos and messages, ways exist to recover information.
- ✦ Trust no one online, not even a best friend or significant other. Today you might be in love with Johnny, but what happens in three weeks when you find out Johnny is secretly texting your best friend? A bad breakup ensues, he starts posting your personal photos, and your secrets are spilled in cyberspace.
- ✦ Dangerous criminals use social media and the Internet to target young victims. Do not trust anyone you meet online, and assume predators can access your digital footprint.
- ✦ Schools, colleges, employers, and parents of friends monitor social media. Anything you say or do online can and will

be used against you. Instead of YOLO (you only live once), adopt LWNR as your Internet slang: live with no regrets.

✦ Let your children know you will not tolerate inappropriate cyber behavior directed at other people. We talk a lot about how to prevent our own children from becoming cyber victims. But also teach your children to use the same courtesy online you expect from them in the physical world.

Did you know parents can be held legally responsible for what their kids do online? Say you give your child a phone, and he or she exchanges inappropriate pictures with friends. Technically, you own the phone, and the phone now contains child pornography. Do not discount the risk you assume when you allow your children online.

Do not have this conversation once and cross it off your parenting checklist. One of my friends, whose teenager constantly acts out online, said to me, "I talked to him, but he keeps doing the same things." Do not expect your children to quickly master online safety; after all, they are kids. But as I said to my friend, "Wake up! Change tactics."

Take the attitude that there are no second chances in cyberspace. If your child repeats unsafe behavior, shut it down. Revoke their Internet privileges, cancel services, double down on family rules. Period.

Staying as open and honest as possible with kids about the potential dangers of social media platforms, like cyber-bullying and identity theft, continues to be an important dialogue. As sophisticated as people may feel, no one is immune to making missteps online, like accidentally revealing private information or confiding personal details to online "friends," who they don't really know.

PRIVACY VERSUS PROTECTION

Digital surveillance of their kids makes some parents feel uncomfortable. If you think children should have total privacy, and you refrain from monitoring digital devices, I have a few questions for you:

+ If your child's online activities could result in your child being suspended from school, or even arrested, do you want to find out after the fact?
+ If your child reveals dangerous behavior online, do you want the chance to keep your child safe?
+ If cyber stalkers and slime balls monitor your child's communications, why not do the same?

Parents should measure the trust and independence they want for their children against safety and caution. Rather than feeling like you are invading their privacy, commit to the idea that you are protecting them.

CYBER TOOLS FOR PARENTS

Concepts aside, here are concrete actions you can take to keep children safe online:

Make sure your kids do not have administrator access on any electronic device. Eliminating administrator access means kids cannot clear cookies or delete browser history. And remember that kids are smart, I mean, really smart. Do what you can to lock down and monitor their systems, but the bottom line is, some kids will still find a way to cover their tracks. A clear browser cache, which means browsing history has been deleted, should set off an instant alarm that they are up to something, something they want to hide.

Periodically, and unannounced, use your kids' electronic devices. Observe the ads that appear for clues about where your kids have been online. This is one of the easiest and best ways to monitor your children's online activity. Websites leave cookies, which generate advertising. If you see ads for inappropriate products, your kids are probably visiting inappropriate websites.

What's good for your gadget is good for Junior's, too. Any device you purchase or pass down to your children should maintain the same levels of privacy and security that you employ for your own new gadget. Make sure to update antivirus software on laptops and install a virtual private network (VPN) on mobile devices that may access the Internet over public WiFi.

Switch into lockdown mode. The Internet is a vast place, and younger children surfing it for the first time are bound to get lost—sometimes in scary places. Set up basic parental controls on any device you give to your child—especially to kids younger than age ten. Turn off location services that may track the whereabouts of your kid's phone or tablet (although you might want to use an application that allows YOU to track your children). Enable options to require passwords before completing in-app purchases in order to avoid accidental charges during gameplay. Limit or eliminate data usage and restrict incoming and outgoing calls to approved numbers.

If a device does not have parental controls built in, it may allow you to create multiple user profiles that can be restricted to using specific applications. Third-party software downloads also help monitor and manage kids' ability to visit certain websites you have deemed inappropriate.

Keep tabs on their browser tabs. Rules about limiting screen time are typically structured around minutes and hours, but you may find it's just as important to keep tabs on content. Be aware of what sites or applications your children visit and download from. For younger children, make sure at least one parent is present (and paying attention) when devices are used.

Keep devices and charging stations in common areas. Good habits are learned over time and conditioned by the environment. If your children can only use and charge electronic devices in public areas of the home, where adults can supervise activities, it is less likely they will run into trouble online. Instead of Big Brother watching, he is just nearby, and that is often all it takes to encourage proper behavior. Encourage children to use devices in common areas, and make it inviting. After dinner in my home, the kids and I all take our laptops into the kitchen and work together. This also encourages interaction, and if they get stuck, they can ask questions.

Designate when electronic devices can be used— and when they cannot be used. Countless studies urge parents to limit children's screen time. The most convincing argument to do so is the negative effect light exposure from screens has on sleep patterns. Use science to your advantage, and define the times of day your children can hop on a tablet or computer. My children are banned from devices until homework is done, and right before bedtime. Lead by example and refrain from device use at the same time. You might be surprised at how easy this becomes when it is part of a routine. If you are really adventurous, try forgoing electronics for a full day or weekend, and schedule some quality family time. Schedule a family game night. Build a family atmosphere and communication that cannot be disrupted by cyberspace.

One last note about parental controls: Remember, that point I keep hammering about nothing being 100 percent secure? The same idea applies to parental controls, especially with older kids. Teenagers will find ways around the safety devices you install. At a certain point, parental controls become less useful, and you move into a new stage where you trust your children, but still monitor their behavior.

DO AS I SAY AND AS I DO

Perhaps the most advisable way to teach kids about keeping themselves and their devices safe is to lead by example. Examine your own online behaviors and make sure you set the best standards for your children to follow.

Talk about social media etiquette with your teens and explain the importance of privacy and security among all your family members.

If you make Internet rules as a family, remember to follow them yourself.

The Internet is here to stay. Helping your children develop a healthy relationship with it has become a big part of being a responsible parent.

To all of the parents who think they do not have to worry about their kids doing something inappropriate online: wake up. Children are awesome, but they will make mistakes. Be ready, so you can protect them.

PREDATORS THRIVE IN CYBERSPACE

Crimes against children gain a new dimension on social media and in cyberspace. When I talk with parents, I show them innocuous-looking profiles from various social media sites, and ask how many of them would allow their children to communicate with these people online. A lot of people raise their hands. Then I reveal the sixteen-year-old into Taylor Swift and horseback riding is a thirty-six-year-old dirtball, arrested seven times for targeting under-age children.

Silence.

A child predator can operate in stealth online, as sadly, many children are not properly educated or monitored when it comes to cyberspace. Some school curriculums now cover basics of online safety, but nothing replaces the one-on-one interaction between an adult and child discussing cyber dangers-in-disguise. The strategies discussed in this chapter will not only teach children how to safeguard themselves, but will also provide a safety net if they falter.

According to The Center for Missing and Exploited Children®, most online predators are not pedophiles. Instead of targeting very young children, cyber criminals are on the prowl for vulnerable teenagers. Predators shower victims with attention and build trust before committing vile crimes, including child sex trafficking. Please, please, please emphasize to your children they should never physically meet anyone they first met online, at least not without a parent or other trusted adult present.

We do not need to scare children, but instead meet them at their maturity level to frankly discuss why cyber safety needs to be taken so seriously. Children are trusting. Online predators know how to find vulnerable children online, slowly build trust and then move in to commit truly terrible crimes. Cyberspace creates a perfect storm: innocent children and truly disgusting criminals.

It can happen to your child. If you take that frightening idea to heart, it will serve as your child's best defense. An alert parent or guardian is key to keeping kids safe in cyberspace.

THE DATING GAME

The blush of a new love can transform just about anyone into, well, a fool. It might seem out of place to talk about online dating after focusing mostly on children, but the Internet arena of love is a place where adults tend to let down their guard and act like children.

People who date online want to look as attractive as possible, and they often share personal information about careers, desires, hobbies, and more. Cyber criminals bank on the idea love is blind, and use dating sites to find potential victims.

If the adversary's goal is identity theft, digital dating profiles provide a great way to find targets and gather personal information. Think about the last time you forgot a password, and the application asked you to name your first pet, your hometown, or your favorite sports team. Where might you find that type of information about somebody else? You get it now.

Daters often flaunt finances online, which result in a heavenly combination for cyber criminals—the wealthy and lonely lovebird. Remember that every detail you reveal could be noted and used by someone with criminal intentions.

Be careful and use common sense online: do not lose your wallet or your identity or your head when you're hoping to lose your heart.

PROTECT YOUR DIGITAL PERSONA

Stalkers and predators aside, cyberspace visitors often perpetrate painful acts upon themselves because they do not think before they act.

I frequently ask my kids: when you look back in a year, will you be glad you posted that information online? Employers and universities routinely research an applicant's online presence. It happens. Job seekers and students routinely lose out on great jobs or college admissions because they posted foolish material online.

A friend's daughter wondered why she did not receive a job offer after a terrific interview. That night I went home, looked at her social media accounts, and found this post:

> *"Awesome interview and looking forward to the new job. The office manager is a little creepy but I should have minimal interaction with the weirdo."*

If your jaw hit the table as you read this, you can start to imagine my facial expression as a cybersecurity professional.

Another friend's daughter even had her college acceptance rescinded because her online behavior, post-acceptance, was deemed to violate the school's personal code of conduct. Her devastated parents defended their daughter's right to free speech, but colleges, clubs, employers, and landlords also have rights. As long as consequences are not based upon discrimination, people can, and will, use online material to judge personal character.

Her parents cried, "Why did nobody warn us?" I am warning parents now: our children's online behaviors now are the foundation of their cyber persona for years to come. Help your children build carefully.

READY, SET, GO!

Most parents did not grow up in a digital world, so they are still learning, too. Teach your children about cyber safety, and you will also be protecting yourself. Never be afraid to ask for help, but also investigate which sources you can trust. Own your responsibility for cyber safety, and instill it in your children.

Approach children as their ally in cyberspace; you are not trying to get them in trouble, rather you are trying to save them from trouble. If you find something concerning or dangerous, explain why and work on a solution to change behaviors moving forward. You keep your children safe now, and instill children with good habits that will last a lifetime.

Here is what you need to remember to earn your cybersecurity black belt:

+ Research and understand how your children use cyberspace. Look at their devices to see which applications they use and what websites they visit.
+ Follow your children on social media. This point is non-negotiable, no matter how embarrassing your kids might find it.
+ Talk frequently to your kids about cyberspace. Need some conversation starters?
  - Everything you do online can be made public.
  - There is no delete button.
  - Trust no one online. Whether by accident or by malice, your digital secrets can be exposed.
  - Predators lurk online.
  - Schools and employers monitor social media and can use it against applicants.
  - Just as you do not want your children to be cyber bullied, you will not tolerate them behaving as cyber bullies.
+ Parents can be held responsible for crimes their children might commit in cyberspace.

✦ Do not be afraid to revoke or limit digital privileges. You are protecting your children.

✦ Never allow your children to have administrator access to any device. This limits their ability to circumvent the parental controls you put in place.

✦ If a child's browsing history is deleted, take that as a sign they are hiding something from you.

✦ Spot-check the ads appearing on your children's devices; it will give you important clues about sites your children visit online.

✦ Make sure to update antivirus software on laptops and install a virtual private network (VPN) on mobile devices that may access the Internet over public WiFi.

✦ Learn what parental controls are available on your devices, and customize access for your children. Limit location services and in-app purchases, and restrict incoming and outgoing communication. Maintain data usage limits.

✦ Get creative when devices do not have parental controls built-in. Create different user profiles, placing strict limits on the profiles used by children.

✦ Third-party software downloads manage kids' ability to visit certain websites you deem inappropriate.

✦ An adult should always be in close proximity when younger children go online.

✦ Place devices and charging stations in common areas.

✦ Set a schedule for when electronic devices can be used. Consider designating certain days, or even a whole weekend, as "electronics-free."

✦ Parental controls are less effective with teenagers, who will look for ways around limits.

+ Model appropriate cyber behaviors and habits for your children.
+ Never, ever forget that the slimiest criminals around thrive on cyberspace's anonymity, looking for young targets.
+ Remind your children that their personal reputations also live online. Teach children to view their cyber behaviors through the lens of an educator, friend, and employer.

CHAPTER 8

DIGITAL CONVERGENCE OR DIGITAL DIVIDE?

I *often refer to our physical world as the real world, and cyberspace is, of course, a virtual world. But what happens when you can no longer differentiate between those two planets?*

THE DIGITAL REVOLUTION

The changes wrought by the digital revolution are staggering; at times, I hardly recognize the world we live in.

I grew up going to Blockbuster on the weekend to rent a VHS movie, before stopping by Borders to pick up a new book. Both retailers were large, successful companies with one minor issue. They did not foresee the digital revolution and did not adapt; both filed for bankruptcy.

Now I stream my movies and read books on a tablet. Both consumers and businesses must adjust to digital innovation or risk being left behind.

There is one segment of the population undaunted by change. Evil forces adapt quickly to new technologies. The cyber crime revolution is moving at warp speed.

DIGITAL CONVERGENCE

As technological capabilities advance, the lines blur between our physical world and cyberspace. New automobiles purchased today carry more computers and networking cable than large organizations in the early 1980s. Self-driving cars cruise some city streets, and your

next fast-food burger may be delivered via drone. Technology is taking over the mundane tasks of human existence.

Most people over forty did not grow up with technology. Their children and the next generation have always utilized technology and recognize it as an integral part of their lives. In general, the tech generation adapts faster and more easily to digital innovation than most adults and teachers.

But risk accompanies the all-consuming, blind faith many of this new generation put in technology, making them easy targets for cyber catastrophes. If we want to protect our families, our children, and our students, we need to understand the consequences of the digital age.

Many of us actually spend more time in the digital world than the real world. Just keep track for one day how much time you spend online, in front of your computer, versus how much you physically talk and interact with people. The difference can be downright scary. I know I have days where I spend eight hours straight in front of a keyboard, with minimal or even no direct human interaction.

One afternoon, my daughter had some friends over to the house. They sat inches away from each other on the couch, texting back and forth for an hour. Finally I took their phones away. For five minutes they did not know what to do, but within thirty minutes, they were laughing and having fun.

The challenge is to use technology to make us better humans, without losing what makes us human.

LOSING TOUCH WITH REALITY

In my experience, the moment most people put their hands on the keyboard, they lose all common sense. If someone walked up to you in the real world and asked for your bank account information, you would not give it to them. Even if they said they worked for the bank, you would refuse. So why would anyone reply to an email from someone claiming to be a bank, requesting account information?

I spend very little personal time on social media, though of course, I follow my children online. On the other hand, to stay up-to-date, I spend a lot of professional time on social media—monitoring platforms, tracking functionality, and observing what people post.

The question I ask people, do you want to be a Kim Kardashian or a Bill Gates? Do you want to expose your personal life? Or do you want to be respected for your accomplishments and quietly enjoy the fruits of your labor?

Kardashian fans, I am not saying fashion is unimportant. I am saying I do not want to be famous because my secrets were accidentally exposed. There is definitely something to learn from

Gates, one of the most brilliant minds of our generation. Live your private life in private, not in public.

Cosmopolitan magazine reached out to me once for an interview. I skeptically returned the phone message, because come on, what cyber geek actually gets quoted in Cosmo? In light of all the news about political and celebrity cybersecurity hacks, the reporter wanted to give readers advice for protecting personal electronic devices.

Sometimes I speak before I think, so the first security tip I offered was, "Never take nude photos." Broken record moment: there are no secrets in cyberspace.

ARTIFICIAL INTELLIGENCE

Is there a difference between being smart versus intelligent? I am not talking about a score on an IQ test, but about the human ability to reason.

Computers map DNA, predict the weather, power global financial transactions, and beam precise navigational assistance from outer space. The ability of digital innovations to quickly follow and execute instructions often exceeds the capabilities of the human brain. Computers are very smart. But the ability to interpret, improvise, and apply knowledge is what constitutes intelligence. Computers are still working on that part.

Go back to the example of the autonomous car. It will have its setbacks, but self-driving technology is here to stay. However, I argue that a vehicle on artificial-intelligence autopilot cannot account for every human factor simply because it is not human.

Artificial intelligence (AI) can create economic efficiencies. The monetary cost of a high-speed chip and some circuit boards is often less than a flesh-and-blood human acting in the same capacity. AI can also protect flesh and blood, sending a robot to do hazardous jobs such as finding and defusing bombs.

Credit card companies and banks use AI to ferret out fraud, detecting unusual transactions and patterns. Those follow-me ads discussed in earlier chapters use rudimentary AI. Security services, energy-saving devices, and online customer support also rely on computer-generated knowledge.

But as the quote that started this chapter suggests, responsible technologists should ensure humans, and not computers, stay in charge, because there are some things that just cannot be replaced by technology.

VIRTUAL REALITY

Virtual reality (VR) is software and other computer technologies that simulate environments where users can interact with virtual surroundings. Used in applications like video games, consumers engage via sensors fitted into helmets, visual displays, and wearable items such as gloves. If you have never tried it, you should. Love it or hate it, it is a technology not to be missed.

Virtual reality can put gamers behind the wheel of a racecar, or train new surgeons to perform complicated medical procedures without the risk of harming patients. Applied, VR can be entertaining or potentially lifesaving.

Have you ever talked to a blind date on the telephone and excitedly set out for a night on the town, only to be bitterly disappointed when you reach the restaurant? You used your own type of VR to build a picture of your date, and now you can see the potential dangers of VR technology. Once again, replacing real world experiences with technology has its limitations.

Related to virtual reality is augmented reality. Augmented reality places digital objects in the real world.

The Pokémon GO craze that tore across the globe in the summer of 2016 is an example of augmented reality. The game projected digital characters into a user's landscape. I never did catch a Mewtwo, did you?

Retailers use augmented reality to show customers how a garment looks on them or how a new couch will look in your living room.

JUST BECAUSE WE CAN

The concerns surrounding artificial intelligence lead to another important question. Just because we can create technology, should we? I will sidestep the ethical debate and instead look at some technological advances of questionable value.

The biggest emerging technology catchphrase this decade is Internet of Things, or IoT. Think of IoT as embedding interactive technology in everyday objects and processes to enhance product value and performance. IoT, or smart technology, is often incorporated into what is being called wearables, like pedometers.

Fitness trackers, wireless medical devices, infant bedding that monitors respiration, thermostats, and home security systems are first-wave IoT technology offering practical and measurable benefits.

Another new IoT invention, the interactive hairbrush "listens" to hair during brushing, analyzing hair health characteristics such as frizziness and breakage. I think the basic principles of capitalism will decide if the world needs an IoT hair gadget.

We can do almost anything with technology, but not all ideas add significant value to our lives.

When considering an IoT device, ask yourself, what will you gain from that application?

IoT technology relies on fundamentally strong cybersecurity measures. Cyber criminals can exploit information gleaned from IoT devices—data such as user location and passwords. Or did you see the television show in which a politician's pacemaker was hacked? It might not be as far-fetched as you think.

All remote access and user-friendly technology adds tremendous flexibility and functionality to our lives, but the same functions and features also simultaneously represent security risks. As you enjoy and employ the newest and coolest tech, just pause and think and ask yourself, what do I gain and what do I lose? It is absolutely great that you can open your garage door from anywhere in the world, but that remote access also means an adversary can potentially do the same thing. Be very aware; be very careful.

WHAT WE LOSE

If all of your digital technology went away, how would that impact your life? Beyond losing the human factor, overreliance on technology can limit the use of critical thinking skills.

Catholic schools have long been famous for emphasizing legible and precise handwriting. But national Common Core education standards do not require instruction in cursive handwriting.

I have listened to more than one child lament over studying for spelling tests, "because spell-check fixes everything anyway." As emphasis shifts from mastering basic computation skills to learning mathematical processes, some students are even allowed to use calculators on math tests. Will handwriting and math skills become lost arts?

According to a UCLA study[1], multitasking enabled by technology may hinder deeper critical analysis and comprehension. The research examined more than fifty studies focusing on learning and technology. One study analyzed by UCLA looked at Internet access in the classroom, and compared students who used the web during lectures against students who did not. Non-surfers performed better than surfers on tests based upon those lectures.

I also want to point out this study does find value in classroom technology. The researcher advocates a balance between traditional and nontraditional teaching techniques. Again, it comes down to balance.

What is technology costing us, in terms of brainpower? Let's stay alert and intentional as we charge into the new frontiers of smart devices.

WHEN IT MAKES SENSE

If I believed technology had no value, I would not have a job. I love technology. Nothing makes me happier than taking apart any device, so I can learn how to put it back together again.

We see every day the value that technology adds to life. A connected factory increases manufacturing efficiencies. A connected home reduces its carbon footprint with energy savings. Medical monitors improve healthcare outcomes.

Who would have ever thought the biggest taxi service in the United States would not own a single car? Uber utilizes technology to organize the masses and makes a ton of money while doing it. Could a ridesharing service be such a success without all of the various technologies used by Uber? Not likely.

I love my fitness tracker; I need the Internet to connect with my colleagues; and I wholeheartedly approve of the idea my doctor can practice using virtual reality before she practices on me. I drive on roads monitored electronically for traffic, base my clothing decisions on a forecast generated in cyberspace, and with three kids, my credit card is like an extension of my hand. I might not always recognize the digital world we live in, but I cannot imagine living anywhere else. I just want consumers to exercise caution.

READY, SET, GO!

No doubt, digital innovations create new opportunities to improve lives. It is easy to talk about all of the positive effects of technology, but we must also consider the potential downside of new inventions. Just like in the physical world, we need an embedded level of security and human intelligence to survive in the digital world.

Here is what you need to remember to earn your cybersecurity black belt:

✦ The digital revolution has already reinvented how you live your life. In fact, cyber innovations will probably reinvent your reality several more times over the course of your lifetime.

✦ Lines blur between the physical world and the cyber world. Be a human who uses technology, not a technical human.

✦ Do not let cyberspace draw back the curtain on your private life.

✦ Artificial intelligence (AI) is the next uncharted galaxy in cyberspace. Self-driving cars are just the beginning.

✦ Virtual reality is not real.

✦ The Internet of Things might make anything possible. But should everything be possible?

✦ Digital technology cannot replace everything. The world's most powerful processor is still the human brain.

[1] Patricia M. Greenfield, "Technology and Informal Education: What Is Taught, What Is Learned," Science 323 (2009) 69-71, accessed January 11, 2017, doi: 10.1126/ science.1167190.

CHAPTER 9

IS IT TIME TO BECOME AMISH?

*"It is desirable that a man live in all respects so
simply and preparedly that if an enemy take the
town . . . he can walk out the gate empty-handed
and without anxiety."*
                    —Henry David Thoreau, Walden

LIFE, SIMPLIFIED

When I give interviews or deliver keynotes, I am sometimes
pushed to reveal the secret to foolproof cybersecurity. There actually
is one way, I pause as I reply, to be 100 percent secure. Forgo all
modern conveniences. Yes, like the Amish.

The Amish and Mennonites are Christian groups that carefully
limit and manage the use of modern inventions. More traditional

orders even prohibit the use of electricity. But progress is steamrolling a path even through these communities. Increasingly, some Amish and Mennonite people are using technology such as refrigerators, cell phones, and even basic computers.

But even the Amish are no longer 100 percent secure. The Amish pay taxes, and many use modern healthcare resources. Technology use is slowly spreading in those rural communities. The Amish do exist in digital databases across the United States. Even if you abstain from email, texting, or the Internet, you likely have a job, pay taxes, or see a doctor. Your personally identifiable information (PII) is stored on computer servers and can be hacked. It is not always your direct activity that puts you at risk.

BEFORE YOU CUT THE CORD

I am a technology advocate, and I cannot advise people to give it up. Think of digital innovation in terms of improved health outcomes, education, communication, entertainment, and all of the many more ways technology enriches the human life.

Driving less could minimize the chances of getting in accident, but you are not going to give up your car just to be safe. But maybe you should drive a little less. Likewise, reducing the amount of data that you store and the amount of time that you use the Internet is good advice that should not be taken lightly. You still can use the Internet. Take measures to reduce your exposure in cyberspace; do not hide from it.

BEYOND YOUR CONTROL

The concepts of cybersecurity and personal security can be frustrating if not completely overwhelming. And now, despite all of this advice about controlling your own actions, I am telling you that your personal cybersecurity is beyond your control. You can do everything right, but ultimately many third parties, like the government or businesses you frequent, also host personal information about you. Every location that stores data about you represents a potential point of compromise.

In late 2016, Yahoo announced a breach in which more than a billion user records were compromised, and terrifyingly, the story quickly blew over. I am still flabbergasted. I know these things will happen, but we should never accept security breaches as the norm.

Internet users, not Yahoo, now live with the aftermath of their information or identity being compromised. Maybe Yahoo will face some fines or a lawsuit, but the company can handle it. Consumers, on the other hand, are left with the long-term repercussions of entrusting their information to an insecure third party.

DEE SNIDER IS A SMART MAN

I am a product of the 1980s, and I love the music of that decade. I especially love Twisted Sister and their classic, rabble-rousing, fight song "We're Not Gonna Take It." Lead singer and the song's writer, Dee Snider, nails it. We're not gonna take it; we will no longer meekly accept third-party data breaches.

We have to stop raising our tolerance level for compromise. Cybersecurity will stagnate until we hold private and public sectors accountable in cyberspace. Until then, companies will continue to make security a low priority.

If a third-party Internet service does not provide proper functionality, and the application repeatedly crashes, we find a new service. Yet when a provider fails to implement security and our records are compromised, we

keep using them. The next time you hear about a mega breach and get frustrated, just remember: you get what you tolerate. If you tolerate poor security, you will get poor security.

If consumers unite and put a few organizations out of business after a cyber breach, security will become a top priority. Until that happens, consumers should resign themselves to the repercussions of inadequate cybersecurity because they are letting companies get away with it.

MAY I HAVE THIS DANCE?

My taste in music might be a little eclectic. Another favorite song of mine is "The Dance" by Garth Brooks. Cybersecurity really is a dance where you strive for a balance. On the one foot (as I keep saying), infallible cybersecurity is impossible. Standing on the other foot, we cannot accept massive security breaches as the new normal. It sounds contradictory, but there must be a tension between the two positions.

If an organization implements robust security, quickly detects a breach, and minimizes consumer impact, that might be the point where we strike the right balance. The golden triangle of successful security: deploy strong defenses, swiftly detect problems, and control the damage.

Many high-profile breaches result from sloppy security, ignoring industry-accepted practices, or even violations of internal security policies. The sad truth is that some companies do weigh the costs of cybersecurity against its benefits, and they choose profits over your protection. I have seen it.

Even worse are the companies that were compromised for long periods of time and failed to detect the problem. When a breach occurs, it can take months, if not years, to come to light. We have established that compromises will happen. But third parties should have proper detection protocols to catch breaches in a timely manner, with the ultimate goal of controlling damage.

BREACHES IN THE NEWS

One of the big misconceptions that we have as a society is that the reason an organization is in the news is because they have had a cybersecurity breach. That is not true. The real reason the company makes the news is because they failed to contain and control the breach. If an organization got compromised and they had 1,000 records stolen, that loss is not newsworthy. What makes the breach newsworthy is when you start adding many zeros after the number, and the loss becomes millions and billions of records.

The problem today with both organizations and individuals is not that they get compromised, but that they fail to detect the breach in a timely manner. Depending on which report you read, most people are compromised for an average of twenty-two months before they detect the breach. Just think about that for a moment: most people's computers and accounts are compromised for almost two years before they realize it. Therefore the probability that you are compromised today, and do not realize it, is very, very high.

These undiscovered breaches are why one simple but effective way to protect yourself is to either rebuild your computer or buy a new one every twelve to eighteen months. As prices continue to drop, computers are becoming inexpensive enough that they really need to be considered almost as disposable devices. Devices that, after a given period of time, are no longer safe and should be replaced by a new model.

TIP OF THE ICEBERG

Only a small percentage of breaches make the news. What you read and hear about does not paint a complete picture.

Many breaches never get reported or are too small to catch the attention of a news editor looking for a tantalizing headline. If 100,000 records are stolen, it barely registers as a blip on the public radar screen. But if you are one of the 100,000, the consequences can be earth shattering.

Just like the tip of an iceberg above the water line—and the unknown ice mass below the water that can cause serious damage—only a miniscule fraction of our nation's cybersecurity problems are reported and known. Security professionals agree not all attacks are caught, and no one really knows how much is being missed.

YOU ARE IN THE RISK MANAGEMENT BUSINESS

Life is about weighing consequences and making choices. Most of us have been doing this for so long, we do not even realize it. We look at the traffic lights before crossing a street. We test the warmth of a cup of coffee before taking a sip. Or we call for a cab to get home after enjoying a few drinks at a party. And even with all these efforts, we cannot completely eliminate risk; it may turn out that the taxi driver has a terrible driving record. Still, it was the best decision, and you did reduce risk by making that call.

We need to develop "street smarts" for cyberspace. When you were younger and started driving, you knew to be careful because you had just learned how to drive—you did not yet have experience on the road. Over the years, as you gained experience, you may have become less wary, maybe even less careful. The thing is, even though we're adults, everyone is a "new driver" in cyberspace. Everyone is inexperienced, relative to the age of digital innovation.

Problems arise because users zip around the information super highway like they have been driving for thirty years, but this road is still under construction. We are all navigating a learning curve. Meanwhile, the adversary is very skilled, and unfortunately, has the upper hand.

MANAGE YOUR SECURITY LIKE YOUR HEALTH

Many people understand the value of their health and that same mindset can be applied to how cybersecurity works.

If someone claims to be 100 percent healthy, they are naïve. The goal of exercise and healthy eating is not to achieve perfection and to live forever, but rather, the goal is to build up our immune systems to reduce the risk of getting sick and to minimize the symptoms and long-term consequences of an illness.

Success in health comes in reducing the frequency of illness and minimizing the impact it has on our lives. If someone occasionally gets sick, they are not labeled "weak" or basically unwell. Meanwhile, if a person gets sick every week and requires hospitalization, they may be considered not only weak but also basically unhealthy.

This same analogy applies to security, especially cybersecurity. If someone says they are 100 percent secure, it is just as naïve as saying they are never going to get sick. We need to recognize that security is all about reducing the risk of getting hacked and minimizing the consequences when an adversary is successful in an attack.

Success in cybersecurity comes in reducing the frequency of hacks or breaches and minimizing the impact on our lives. If we want zero impact, we become Amish, which is not a viable solution for most people. Sadly, most people go the other extreme, acting carelessly in their cyber habits. We must adopt a different cyber lifestyle because the more we are careful, the more protected we can be—all while still enjoying the benefits of an electronic life.

INSURANCE IS YOUR FRIEND

Cyber threats are growing severe, and I hope my advice will help protect you for many years. But my guess is cyber insurance for individuals and families will become a lot more commonplace.

Cyber insurance is brand new, and like any insurance, its goal is to reduce highly hazardous or uncertain areas of life to an acceptable level of risk. Most of us have home insurance, life insurance, and automobile insurance. Depending on what you do on the Internet, it may be time for you to start thinking about cyber insurance, too.

Today, when a company is breached and your personal information is compromised, that third party (the company that was breached) will usually offer a year of free credit monitoring. Better than nothing, but credit monitoring only alerts you to potential problems. It does not fix the problem. Essentially, breached organizations hire a company to tell you when your identity is stolen. The more appropriate response would be to offer cyber insurance or to cover any financial losses customers incur.

Standard practices—and the customer services offered by compromised companies—will not change until consumers demand it. If enough people ask for it, we can effect changes that will actually help consumers. And until then, personal cyber insurance may be the answer to reducing individual risk.

TAKE ACTION NOW

You might wish you knew a lot of this information ten years ago, and you're right, ideally ten years ago would have been a perfect time to think about cybersecurity. But when is the next best time? NOW. Do not complain about cybersecurity, do something about cybersecurity.

Even I—with all my experience as an intelligence officer, corporate executive, and professor dedicating my entire career to information security—can make a bad decision and utilize an organization with poor security. But I implement strategies to reduce my exposure in the event of a breach.

I hold multiple email accounts for different purposes. I never store all of my information in the same place. I keep my software and hardware up-to-date. I back up my files. I weigh the risks of being online against what I gain from cyberspace. No, I do not want to be compromised. But when it happens, I will be prepared.

I hope by this point these strategies seem simple and straightforward, because that is the whole idea. I recognize that if I gave you super-complicated methods for being secure, most people would not follow them or would make more mistakes. I spend a lot of my time researching and brainstorming ways to make security as simple as possible. The easier a solution is to implement, the more effective it will be overall.

READY, SET, GO!

Controlling your own destiny does not mean you can carefully dictate everything that will happen in your life. To me, it means you are prepared for almost anything, and you alone control how you react to life's curve balls.

Arm yourself with new information, make better decisions, and recognize cyberspace is a very scary place. It is never too late to change.

Here is what you need to remember to earn your cybersecurity black belt:

✦ Forgoing all technology is not the answer to keeping yourself safe in cyberspace. Balance a digital lifestyle with the risks you encounter online.

✦ Many cyber dangers are beyond your control, such as when a major email server is hacked or a credit card database is compromised.

✦ Do not accept data breaches as the norm. Insist that your vendors dedicate more resources to cybersecurity. Companies must reduce the amount of time it takes to find breaches, and they must patch problems at a faster rate.

✦ Only a fraction of all hack attacks are ever discovered. An even smaller fraction of incidents are disclosed to consumers.

✦ Cyber breaches often go undetected for long periods of time. As the price of personal electronics drops, consider replacing devices every twelve to eighteen months, so you are starting off with a fresh, and hopefully uncompromised, slate.

✦ Personal cybersecurity is all about risk management. Weigh the pros and cons of everything you do in cyberspace, and find your acceptable level of risk. Make wise decisions and you can reduce the chances you will suffer from a data breach and contain the potential damage to your life.

✦ If protection is your paramount concern, consider cyber insurance. Just as consumers buy coverage for their physical health, you can purchase protection for your cyber persona.

✦ Set up and maintain multiple email accounts for different cyber purposes. If one account is hacked, only the data associated with that specific account will be compromised.

CHAPTER 10

SAFETY IN A DIGITAL WORLD

"Our lives are a sum total of the choices we have made."

—*Wayne Dyer*

A ROAD MAP

Armed with the straightforward advice in this book, you are now equipped to live a healthy lifestyle in cyberspace. Healthy does not mean you will never get sick, but now you can minimize the frequency and impact cyber incidents have on your life. Approach cyberspace with a full awareness, and while incidents will happen, they will be few and far between.

Throughout this book we have looked at tips, tricks, and appropriate ways to approach cyberspace. You now have a road map for staying safe in a digital world. Remember, you must accept responsibility for your life and the actions you take in cyberspace. For all of those strong, powerful people who have made it to this last chapter, we will review the key areas of cybersecurity that will help you control your digital life.

THE DRIVER'S SEAT

As you retool your cyber life, empower yourself with concepts that support smart decision making in the digital world. Take back control from your cyber adversaries:

+ **Security is an afterthought.** With almost all products and services that you buy, functionality drives design and sales processes. Security is tacked on at the end, or added after public pressure surrounds a serious security issue. You should always act under the premise that there is little to no security and always be careful of what you do and what you say.

+ **Turn on security measures.** Even when vendors include robust security in products, it is often turned off by default. Whenever you sign up for a new service, buy a new product, or install a new application, ask yourself, "What security measures are available, and how do I turn them on?" Always verify things are working in a secure manner and never assume they are.

+ **There are no secrets or second chances.** Everything you say or do online is at risk for exposure. Everything. And once your information hits cyberspace, there is no going back. The delete button is better named the "mostly delete" button.

Your digital footprints and fingerprints are proven trails that trace right back to you.

+ **Trust no one.** People are not always who they seem to be online. No foolproof way exists to verify or authenticate online accounts and personas. As we sometimes like to say in the security world, trust but verify. Always be skeptical of any social media request and ask, "Am I certain that I really know anyone in cyberspace?"

+ **The Internet is evil.** Used correctly, the power of the Internet can transform your life. But in the wrong hands, that power can destroy your life. Organized gangs, nation states, and cyber criminals all target you, waiting for the moment you make a mistake that can be exploited. Behind every website, email, attachment, and URL, evil lurks.

+ **Give in to a little paranoia.** A healthy dose of fear and distrust will keep you safe in cyberspace, so go ahead and examine all online activity under the lens of mild paranoia. Ask, could this item be malicious? Who am I really communicating with online? What do I gain by interacting in cyberspace? Use out-of-band verification, such as texting or calling the person who sent you an email, to see if they really did send you something.

Exceptions to every rule, not just digital guidelines, exist. But erring on the side of caution will serve you well. If you check to make sure built-in security measures are active, and they are, you did not hurt yourself or waste any time. Instead, you ensured your digital safety.

Do you know what is really cool about these preventive actions? They are easy to follow, and they are the same models followed by every cybersecurity expert, including myself. It does not have to be hard to protect yourself in cyberspace. There are many security tips and tricks that I have tried throughout the years that have not worked out well or were too hard for people to implement, so I left all of those out. Keep it simple and keep it safe.

CYBER HYGIENE

Many of us entered the wondrous world of cyberspace with little thought about cybersecurity or the dangers that might lurk online. Users are fairly accustomed to installing endpoint security like virus protections and calling it a day.

Such basic measures worked fifteen years ago, but now is the time for all of us to up our game. The number of adversaries online and the damage they cause increases at a staggering rate. While security products and security settings play a critical role in cyber defenses, developing the right mindset fosters proper cyber hygiene. How you act online is your best defense.

Developing proper habits requires discipline, focus, and forced repetition until you automatically perform your new behaviors. As

a child, your parents probably had to remind you, and maybe force you, to brush your teeth, or you would forget to do it. Thanks to persistent parenting, you eventually realized brushing is important. In the beginning, it was work and sometimes required fighting inner demons. But once you did it long enough, it became habit, and now you do it without even thinking about it.

This same logic also applies to cybersecurity. Force yourself to practice proper cyber hygiene for a few months, and good habits will become second nature.

+ **Never click on links in email.** Embedded links in emails are very dangerous, and you should never ever click on a link directly from an email. The seemingly harmless link is a favorite tool of cyber crooks. Always perform a mini risk assessment on every email and confirm that the potential benefits of the email are greater than any risks. If you cannot make that determination, delete the email.

+ **Never open an email attachment.** Email was not designed to be a mechanism for exchanging documents. Since emails can be spoofed, what looks like a legitimate email with a legitimate attachment can actually be fake. Attachments in email might not always be what they appear to be, and instead may hide malicious code that infects systems. If you are going to exchange documents with other entities, use a trusted third-party exchange mechanism, in which both parties provide proper authentication and are verified.

+ **Devise strong passwords.** With many sites, passwords are your first and only line of defense. Make passwords difficult to crack, using a combination of letters, symbols, and numbers. Passwords based on your name or other personally identifiable information are easy for you to remember, and simple for the adversary to break. I recommend paraphrased passwords, based on a pattern of common words or letters that are easy for you to remember, but hard for the adversary to guess. For example, T2saocC! stands for "<u>T</u>ips <u>2</u> <u>s</u>tay <u>a</u>head <u>o</u>f <u>c</u>yber <u>C</u>riminals<u>!</u>"

✦ **Utilize different passwords.** Many people love using the same two or three passwords for every website they visit. Once again, do not underestimate the adversary. They are pretty smart and know to try similar password patterns. If you are still struggling, look at the next tip to provide some relief.

✦ **Use password-vaulting solutions.** You will probably remember the passwords you use on a daily basis. The problem often comes with sites that you might only access once a week or a few times a month. Password-vaulting solutions store all of your passwords but require robust authentication to access those passwords. You just have to remember one password to securely access all of your codes. However, vault passwords can also be compromised. This is why many of these programs utilize alternative forms of authentication, such as a biometric fingerprint, which brings us to our next tip.

✦ **Employ two-factor authentication.** Two-factor authentication requires information in addition to a password to access an account. This is where the fun, science-fiction stuff comes in. Biometric identifications, such as your fingerprint or retina scan, are no longer science fiction fantasies. Two-factor authentication will soon be commonplace.

✦ **Encrypt sensitive information.** If you store or back up sensitive information to the Internet or cloud-based solutions, always locally encrypt the data and then back up the encrypted information. Only encrypted information should be stored remotely. If your virtual storage is compromised, adversaries are left only with encrypted information. Many operating systems and third-party security solutions offer built-in encryption tools that are user friendly, no cyber expertise required.

✦ **Maintain separate email accounts.** Do not put all of your eggs in one cyber basket. Separate email accounts reduce risk of exposure from one source, so take the time to set up and use different emails accounts with different providers for different purposes. I am not saying you need 100 email accounts, but using four or five email addresses is practical and reasonable. If one is compromised, an adversary only gets a fraction of your emails, not all of them.

✦ **Operate different personas.** The concept of separation and reducing losses works for more than email—it relates to all areas of your cyber life. Adopting different personas online can simply mean using two computers; one for accessing the Internet, checking email and surfing the web, and another computer for sensitive applications like banking and taxes. Remember the two most dangerous applications on planet Earth are web browsers and email clients. When those functions are separated, your cyber exposure reduces significantly.

✦ **Control your data.** If we can get right down to the core of the problem, everything in cybersecurity revolves around protecting and controlling access to your critical information. Remember, the difference between a major breach and a minor breach is not the system that was compromised, but the data that was accessed. Identify critical information, keep track of its location, and frequently assess the security measures you have in place to protect it.

✦ **Never electronically share sensitive information.** Delete all emails requesting your password, credit card number, or other sensitive information. Legitimate vendors, such as your bank, never request personal details via email. Use this same strategy with text and phone calls. If you receive communication claiming to be a bank or credit card company asking for sensitive information, have them verify their identity first. Look for a phone number on the back of your credit card or an account statement, call the company directly to verify the activity, and verbally provide sensitive data.

✦ **Always turn off your computer.** It sounds like a no-brainer, but turn off your devices when you are not using them. When your devices are off, they are not targets. Simple and effective, but something many users fail to do.

✦ **Only post public information online.** The Internet is an open network. Say this out loud twenty times. If you can learn this one rule, you will avoid so many issues, so many fights, and so many problems. Regardless of your security settings, anything posted online has a high probability of being seen by a lot more people than you intended. Act under the premise that everything is public, and you will be in a much more protected position.

✦ **Utilize different credit cards online.** If you shop online, limit the number of sites where you use a credit card. Use several different credit cards spread across sites to make it easier to isolate the source of potentially fraudulent charges. Set low spending limits for your online credit cards to reduce potential losses. Even if the credit card company is left holding the bag, dealing with a compromised credit card is a huge hassle.

Some of these tips will be harder to perform than others, and that is actually a very big warning sign, which may highlight where you are most vulnerable online. If you find one or two of these ideas very challenging, those are probably the areas where you have already developed dangerous cyber habits, and it is time to break the cycle.

If you need motivation, focus on the benefits provided by these healthy cyber rules. Are they foolproof? No. But they offer your best defense against cyber crime.

PARENTING IN CYBERSPACE

No one ever said that being a parent is easy. But the payoff of seeing your child smile, or overcome an obstacle, makes the job worthwhile. Parenting involves a lot of responsibility, and cyberspace only adds to that load.

Taking away a teenager's phone is about as much fun as a root canal without painkiller, but the withdrawal could very well be necessary to keep a child safe. To the other extreme, I can always tell which parents opt out of being a parent on cyberspace, letting their children learn on their own, with no parental discipline or oversight. Those are the children who get into trouble for posting inappropriate content and who are at greater risk for becoming victims of terrible cyber crimes.

Like practicing good cyber hygiene, cyberspace parenting is challenging to learn. But as a parent, follow some simple rules for protecting your children online. With all due respect to debate team members and future lawyers, these points should all be non-negotiable.

+ **Monitor all social media activity.** Follow all of your children's online accounts. Some parents push back on this, maintaining their children deserve privacy. But while some parents might decide not to look for their kids online, teachers, friends, other parents, and potential employers do see what those children are posting. Putting your head in the cyber sand is galactically stupid. Always consider how your children's posts can be used to hurt them, and you will quickly determine if you should intervene.

✦ **Always have access to your child's device.** More precisely, refer to a child's tablet, laptop, or phone as "your device, which you are temporarily allowing your child to use." Unless they are eighteen, paid for the device, cover monthly access charges, and assume all liability for their actions online, the device is not your child's, it is yours. If a child tries blocking access to a device, that should serve as a major warning sign. What are they trying to hide?

✦ **Perform periodic spot-checks.** Enforcement leads to compliance. While some people will follow the rules no matter what, most people are more inclined to do what is right when they know they are being monitored. The same holds true for kids online. Knowing an adult looks over their shoulder also gives children an acceptable way to stand up to peer pressure and act safely online.

✦ **Place devices and charging stations in public locations.** If children can go into their rooms, lock doors, and work on their computers or devices, they are more likely to be tempted by bad behavior or peer pressure. In essence, using devices in private places creates an environment that is very easy for children to find trouble. Place charging stations for all electronics in a public area, like the kitchen. When it is time for bed, the devices stay in that designated area.

✦ **Turn on device location services.** One of the benefits of children having cell phones or other connected devices is we can track and locate them. This is not for spying purposes but for safety purposes. From a parental perspective, there is nothing wrong with using technology to keep your children safe. Fortunately there is a simple fix—decree electronic devices can only be used in the home's public spaces.

+ **Lock devices when necessary.** Owning a mobile phone is a privilege not a right, and privileges can be taken away if rules are broken. Most cell phones can be remotely locked, data plans can be turned off, and contacts can be limited. Because honestly, taking away a child's phone is not always a practical option. I want my kids to be able to reach me whenever they want. Parents should familiarize themselves with security features that allow users to limit how a mobile phone is used. And yes, there have been cases where I took the phone away for an entire week, and we survived.

+ **Check browser history.** Browser history will tell parents where their kids visited on the Internet, but know this, kids are very smart. Remember that the absence of information is information. If I check my child's computer, and the history is deleted, that is an indicator they might be doing something dangerous online. Check the advertisements that appear on children's browsers because those ads are determined in part by the website a user visits and can provide additional clues about online behavior.

+ **Set a schedule.** Many people, especially children, become addicted to electronic devices. To combat digital dependence, set limits on device use. Designate certain times as off-limits for use, such as an hour before bedtime or when children first get home from school.

+ **Plan electronics-free days.** Take electronics scheduling to the next level and completely cut the connection. Once or twice a month, try electronics-free weekends: no mobile phone, texting, or email. Afterwards you will realize how powerful breaking an addiction can be.

Many of these methods will only work if you position them correctly. Here's what will not work: Charge in, tell your children, "We do not trust you, and we are going to spy on you." You love your children and want what is best for them. You are their ally and not their adversary. Instead of engaging them in battle, position the family's cybersecurity policy as teamwork, and create an open environment where parents and children freely communicate about cyberspace.

CYBERSECURITY SELECTIVITY

If you are a skilled craftsperson, you know that you do not use every tool for every project. Some tools are used more often than others, and some tools rarely leave the toolbox. With your cyber toolkit, the more solutions you carry, the better off your security will be. But can you always carry around such a heavy load?

Maybe you pass over protective measures for low-risk items because rigorous security is not practical for that part of your life. You calculate an acceptable level of risk. If you short change safety because it is hard, beware. Keep yourself honest and make choices for the right reasons.

Remember that phrase, "defense in depth"? No single technology or tip will ensure your cybersecurity. If such a method did exist, this book would actually be a five-page paper, and I would need a new job. Fortunately for me (because I have three college educations to pay for), cybersecurity is not that simple. While you do not have to apply every piece of advice I offer, please implement way more than one. Give your defense some real depth.

Achieve a balance between functionality and security: 100 percent security equals zero functionality, and complete functionality translates to no security. Avoid extremes and find the number that makes sense to you.

In my experience, the average user's online security should hang towards 60–70 percent secure. The scary part is most people that I offer cyber "bodyguard" services to are only 10–15 percent secure.

TURN IT ON, TURN IT UP

Even I have had that crazy day where nothing goes my way; I ignore my own advice and click on something dangerous. But even though I slip and click, my defense in depth, with built-in security measures I remembered to turn on, saves the day. While not perfect, basic controls can help protect you and minimize the impact when you do venture into the Twilight Zone.

+ **Antivirus Software.** Antivirus software detects known malicious code and viruses, keeping computers disease-free.
+ **Host-Based Intrusion-Prevention.** While viruses are nasty, other types of malicious code pose more danger. Host-based intrusion-prevention software (HIPS) monitors systems searching for suspicious behavior and blocks questionable actions before a system suffers significant damage.
+ **Application Whitelisting.** Any application that runs or executes on a system carries the potential for harm. While antivirus and intrusion prevention software look for malicious activity, an additional method of protection is to only allow authorized applications to run. Application whitelists designate which verified programs are allowed on a system. If an application is modified, it is no longer allowed access to a device or network. A more complex defensive measure, whitelisting is still something users should know about.
+ **Full Disk Encryption.** If you travel with a laptop, consider encrypting all data on it. If the device is lost or stolen, the information it contains provides no value to an adversary,

unless the encryption can be broken. Protect your personal information in case your device falls into the wrong hands.

✦ **Software Updates**. Vulnerabilities are constantly discovered within software. Keep software up to date and properly patched. Turn on automatic patching in software settings to shorten the amount of time a vulnerability exists on your system.

READY, SET, GOODBYE!

Most authors celebrate the end of a manuscript, and I have a nice bottle of whiskey to open when this book hits the presses. But I am also a little sad because this means our journey together in cyberspace is coming to a close. Even though I have not met many of you in a physical sense, I feel like we have connected in spiritual sense. I care about you, your families, and your companies, and about your long-term success in a digital world.

My passion is to make cyberspace a safer place to live, work, and raise a family. I hope this book accomplishes some of that mission. But look in a mirror and you will see the only person responsible for your cybersecurity.

Embrace the excitement of cyberspace and accept its challenges, too. Arm yourself with the essential tools for making safe choices. Make it a goal over the next three months to invest in your cybersecurity. New routines will morph into safe habits. Be proactive and take control of your destiny.

Be a cyber ninja, and travel the information super highway confidently, and at safe speeds. Now that you have your black belt, use it.

In closing, my digital wish for you:

May your cyber skills rise up to meet you,

May the cyber adversary always be at your back,

May the benefits of the Internet provide you joy,
And your incidents be minor,
And until we meet again,
May God hold you in the palm of His hand.

ABOUT THE AUTHOR

Dr. Eric Cole is an industry-recognized security expert with more than twenty years of hands-on experience in information technology. His work focuses on helping customers identify specific areas of potential compromise and then building dynamic defense solutions that protect their organizations from advanced threats.

An inventor with more than twenty patent applications, Dr. Cole is also a researcher, writer, and speaker. His other books include *Advanced Persistent Threat: Understanding the Danger and How to Protect Your Organization; Hackers Beware: The Ultimate Guide to Network Security; Hiding in Plain Sight: Steganography and the Art of Covert Communication; Network Security Bible,* and *Insider Threat: Protecting the Enterprise from Sabotage, Spying, and Theft.*

Dr. Cole holds a master's degree in computer science from New York Institute of Technology and a doctorate from Pace University, with a concentration in information security. He was a member of the Commission on Cyber Security for the 44th President and is a member of several executive advisory boards. He was inducted into the 2014 Infosecurity Hall of Fame.

Dr. Cole is founder and CEO of Secure Anchor Consulting, which provides state-of-the art security services and expert witness work. He also served as CTO of McAfee and Chief Scientist for Lockheed Martin. Dr. Cole is actively involved with the SANS Technology Institute (STI) and SANS, working with students, teaching, and maintaining and developing courseware. He is a SANS faculty Fellow and course author.